WEYMOUTH

From Old Photographs

WEYMOUTH

From Old Photographs

EDDIE PROWSE

AMBERLEY

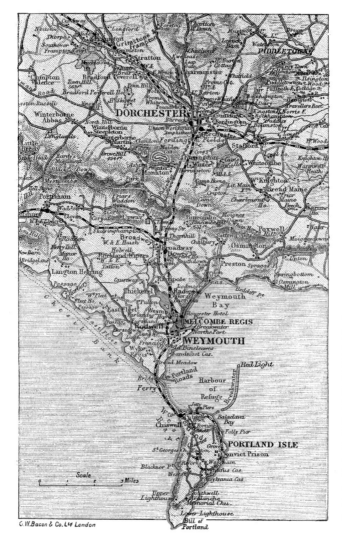

The early 1900s and Portland Breakwater has yet to be completed. The horse barracks located in Lower Bond Street, formerly the cavalry barracks, are indicated. The railway line to Abbotsbury is seen heading away from the junction at Upwey, while the line to Portland is also visible. Surrounding villages and geographical features are marked in great detail.

First published 2014

Amberley Publishing
The Hill, Stroud
Gloucestershire, GL5 4EP

www.amberley-books.com

Copyright © Eddie Prowse, 2014

The right of Eddie Prowse to be identified as the Author of this work has been asserted in accordance with the Copyrights, Designs and Patents Act 1988.

ISBN 978 1 4456 2289 7 (print)
ISBN 978 1 4456 2303 0 (ebook)

British Library Cataloguing in Publication Data.
A catalogue record for this book is available from the British Library.

Typesetting by Amberley Publishing.
Printed in the UK.

Contents

Introduction

Weymouth, a town with a long and fascinating history, originally developed as two distinct settlements either side of the mouth of the River Wey. The Wey is only a short river rising at Upwey, flowing into the wider Radipole Lake and narrowing once more through the Backwater and harbour before reaching the sea. Signs of Stone Age activity have been discovered in the area and it is believed that the Romans used the Wey as far as the north of Radipole Lake, perhaps to reach the hill fort at Maiden Castle. The latter is visible today opposite the modern settlement at Poundbury, Dorchester.

The fortunes of the two communities, Weymouth to the south-west and Melcombe to the north-east, ebb and flow as historical events bring either fortune or disaster. Disputes between the two communities lasted for a number of years and occasionally resulted in violence. This situation continued even after the Charter of Union in 1571 was granted by Elizabeth I.

The Weymouth we know today probably owes much to two factors: the Georgians and the railway. In the mid-1700s, the arrival of Ralph Allen, who also had interests in Bath, resulted in the town becoming a resort for recreation. Allen had royal connections and eventually, in 1789, King George III made his first visit while recovering from illness. The monarch stayed for ten weeks at Gloucester Lodge to avail himself of the supposed curative features of 'taking the waters'. As in Bath and other spas, this practice of drinking and bathing in spa or seawater as a medical treatment was popular at the time. Royal patronage ensured that the practice became established in Weymouth. George was to continue his visits until 1805. The wealthier classes continued to visit after the King's death and there followed a period of steady expansion.

Weymouth was finally connected to the railway network in 1857. As a resort for recreation, the town was the preserve of the wealthy prior to the railway. The expanding Victorian rail network brought the town within easy reach of the inhabitants of expanding cities and towns of the Industrial Revolution. These hard-working people were keen to enjoy their increasing prosperity and spend their leisure time in fresher air than that of the towns and cities. The seaside holiday was born.

By 1850, the science of photography had made huge steps forward and albumen prints from glass negatives became commercially available. They were used to produce permanent images once William Fox Talbot had pioneered the process. The glass negatives continued in use well into the twentieth century, but were eventually replaced with the forerunner of the photographic negatives so recently displaced by today's digital imagery.

The Victorians took to photography with their customary enthusiasm for the new discoveries of the day. Most towns could boast at least one or two photographers, if not more. Weymouth was no exception. Between 1840 and

1930, at least forty photographic businesses were operating in the town, many like Seward or Cumming continuing to record the town and its people well into the mid-twentieth century. Family portraits, buildings or events were all captured by these enthusiastic practitioners. More importantly, it became possible to reproduce these images in volume at lower cost, ideal for use on postcards.

Plain postcards, as a means of communication, first appeared in Austria around 1869, and within twelve months they had reached Britain. Postcards with pictures began to appear a few years later. It was during the Paris Exhibition of 1889 that they became a popular means of sending messages, presumably with pictures of the exhibits.

It was not too long before picture postcards began to appear all over the world. At that time, the address occupied the reverse and any message was usually written alongside or around the view or image on the front. In 1902, Britain was first to introduce a card with a divided back, thus allowing any message and the address to be written on the reverse with a larger image than previously possible on the front.

The years before the First World War have been called the 'Golden Age' of postcards. Photographers covered every conceivable subject, producing popular views and pictures of local and national events. Weymouth's photographers were no exception. Individual camera ownership was in its infancy, so a ready demand existed and collecting postcards soon became a popular pastime.

After the war, the hobby of collecting postcards never regained its earlier popularity and postcards became increasingly associated with the seaside holiday. National publishers concentrating on views of local interest became established, although many local photographers continued to thrive.

I have endeavoured to find cards and photographs from my collection that may not have been seen before; they show a familiar feature from a different viewpoint or capture an event. Even after twenty-five years of collecting, I am still discovering cards or spotting something new in an existing picture. I hope you find something of interest or perhaps an awakening memory.

ARMS OF

SIGILLUM WYLLE DE WAYMOTH ET MELCOMBE REGIS

WEYMOUTH

Early Photographs

The Esplanade

Cartes de Visites (CDVs), similar to those on the following pages, were an early form of pictorial souvenir. Photographed using a glass negative and reproduced as albumen prints, they were then applied to a card (in this case around 3 inches by 2 inches). I believe the photographer is standing approximately where New Street joins the Esplanade. Prominent in this view from around 1865 are the two major hotels: Gloucester Lodge, where George III resided on his visits and, beyond, the white, bow-windowed Stacie's Hotel. The building with the pillars has been long demolished. The small white pillars are linked by chain and lined the promenade.

Georgian Bathing Machines
The original octagonal bathing machines from the Georgian era (with their distinctive roofs) sit alongside the later models (with their pitched roofs). The machines would be wheeled into the water and the bather would descend, having changed into suitable swimwear. Victorian gentlemen in stovepipe hats escort ladies or enjoy the view from a bench. The photographer is using the balcony visible above the pillars of the building in the picture of the Esplanade above. It is low water, and the gentle slope of Weymouth Sands are seen to advantage. This feature of the bay has made it a popular and safe attraction for families. The seaweed is certainly no longer left to accumulate, as seen here. In the distance beyond St John's church, the early property developments at Greenhill can just be seen.

The Pier and Quayside
Standing on the Nothe, the bay, sands and terraces are shown at their best in this print from around the 1870s. This location would remain a favourite with photographers down the years. The work completed in 1860 to improve the original wooden pile pier can be seen. The tramway that brought trains to the harbour ended just to the left of the roundhouse at the end of Devonshire Buildings. The rails were extended on the pier in 1889. The harbour ferryman, still operating today, waits to row customers across the harbour.

Southern Esplanade

A rather nattily dressed gentleman taking in the view of a deserted seafront and sands is captured by the photographer. We can only wonder what the large roller was used for. A wonderful selection of Georgian architecture is shown in the various terraces stretching away towards the harbour. The building with the blank wall behind the roller was demolished in the 1950s; it was part of a terrace among the first to be built facing the sea.

Greenhill Gardens

When looking at this sylvan scene, it is difficult to imagine that it was here that Judge Jeffreys had a gallows erected to execute twelve men who were sentenced to death at the Bloody Assizes. The judge presided over these trials following the Monmouth Rebellion. The poor souls then had their heads and limbs or quarters displayed around the area. The gardens at Greenhill were paid for by Sir Frederic Johnstone in response to a promise made during an earlier election. They were planted in 1872 and the hedges were presumably to provide protection from the sea breezes.

The Royal Hotel

The Royal Hotel is here photographed between 1878 (when the Tea Cabin seen to the left was opened) and 1887. The latter date is when the Jubilee Clock, not seen in this view, was erected. Initially known as Stacie's Hotel, after its original owner, it opened in the 1770s. The large bow-windowed building was a significant seafront feature until 1891, when it was demolished. The change of name occurred in the 1780s in response to the Duke of Gloucester building Gloucester Lodge on an adjacent plot. The large billboard advertises a bazaar at Holy Trinity church, and the American Studio was an early photographic portraiture business.

The Wooden Landing Stage

We return to the harbour and two paddle steamers from the Cosens fleet are moored alongside the pier awaiting the first passengers of the day. The railway has been extended onto the pier, thus enabling us to date this image to around 1890. The wooden landing stage seen in this view was built by Weymouth Corporation with some funding by the Great Western Railway (GWR). It proved immediately beneficial as cargoes increased and were handled more efficiently. Harbour dues rose, enabling the Corporation to clear the debt incurred in building the stage by 1879. In the background, the Georgian terraces provide the backdrop and the bathing machines are in position.

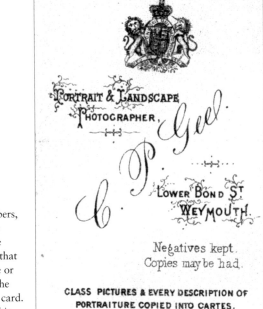

A Group of Workers

Cartes de Visite were produced in vast numbers, and many were views and portraits, but this would appear to be a group of workers. The similar attire of the ladies perhaps indicates that they are all employed in a hotel, guest house or inn. The card is 10 cm by 6 cm in size and the details on the right are on the reverse of the card. Charles Palmer Gee had studios, including this in Lower Bond Street, between 1874 and 1880. Other prolific publishers of CDVs in the town at that time were Edgar Cox, E. Debenham & Co. and Harry Wheeler.

Léon & Lévy

1 - WEYMOUTH. - The Beach - LL.

Donkey and Goat Rides

The view cards produced by Léon & Lévy, distinguished by the 'LL', seem to capture and reflect in a particularly distinctive manner the years when the Victorian era gave way to the Edwardian. Their mastery of the collotype process adds a clarity not found in other similar cards. Cards were produced for France, England and many other countries. Today the Léon & Lévy glass negatives are held by the Roger-Viollet archive in Paris. The ornate carts on the ramp were pulled by goats and one can be seen taking a rest from his labours. The pony rides, operated by the Downton family for many years, were a regular feature of an early summer's evening. They were led back through the town to the stables.

43 *WEYMOUTH. — The Sidney Hall. — LL.*

The Sidney Hall

The quality Léon & Lévy achieved with their photographs and printing process is most obvious in this view of the Sidney Hall. 'Christmas is Coming', declares the poster by its main entrance, probably advertising a Christmas Fayre. The building was a gift to the parish of Holy Trinity and the Church Lads' Brigade from Sir John Groves in memory of his son, Sidney, who died in 1895. It served as a military hospital during the First World War and, following bomb damage in Chapelhay, provided classrooms for the displaced children of Holy Trinity School. It is fondly remembered by several generations as a venue for roller skating and dances. Sadly, it is now demolished and the land is part of a supermarket car park.

The Beach opposite Victoria Terrace

A small family group is enjoying the shingle beach in front of Victoria Terrace with the Burdon Hotel dominating the scene. They are probably watching boats similar to those in the background, which were available for hire. In the distant background, tents that were also available for hire line the beach in front of Brunswick Terrace and towards Greenhill. Given that the cameras used at the time were bulky and obvious, we must assume that most of these views with groups were posed to allow the camera to catch a clear image.

10 *WEYMOUTH. — The Sands. — 11.*

Sand Modellers at Work

The wonderful quality of modelling possible with Weymouth's sand is seen clearly in this picture. What appears to be an oversized squid and a group of horses with a description would eventually be destroyed by the incoming tide. The stonework, known locally as 'breakwater stone', was an attempt to prevent tidal drift removing sand. Today, the drop from the promenade to the sand is considerably reduced and a cast-iron railing runs from this point to an area just beyond the Jubilee Clock.

The Nothe

An unidentified GWR steamer from the Channel Islands service is moored against Weymouth Quay, with a smaller paddle steamer from the Cosens fleet of pleasure boats also tied up alongside. An interesting selection of large and small private sailing boats is moored close to the Nothe Gardens. The small wooden jetty is probably the one used when Nothe Fort was in active military use. A small railway ran alongside a flight of steps known as the Fusee Steps; both were used to move ammunition and stores into the fort. Today, Nothe Fort is a popular tourist attraction with regular historical demonstrations of its former use.

The Cove

Viewed from a point just above the Cove, the weather does not appear at its best, although the young man in the bottom right corner seems happy to sit on a jetty. Across the harbour, an unidentified GWR Channel Islands steamer is tied up with a pair of Cosens paddle steamers at its stern. A small fleet of 'clinker'-built boats (a method of boatbuilding where the edges of the hull planks overlap) were probably all made in boatyards alongside the harbour close to where the photographer is standing.

Steam and Sail

Sail power was beginning to give way to steam around the 1900s when this picture was taken just along from the Cove. The *Alcethi* is unloading cargo onto Trinity Road. Across the harbour alongside Custom House Quay is a sailing ship, which may be a fishing vessel. The small building occupied by Cosens is now part of the building to its right, which is today a restaurant. The George Inn survives and has absorbed the building to its left. The building behind the sailing ship is today occupied by a fish merchant. The Ship Inn has survived and has expanded into the adjacent building. The Royal Oak, with the rounded corner, remains as seen in this view.

9 WEYMOUTH. – Pier Pavilion from Harbour. – LL.

Nothe Parade

Hopefully, the young man has permission to be in one of the boats owned by the Tizard family, although he could have been passing with his companion when the cameraman persuaded him to pose. This is another great view of clinker-built boats moored close to a small boatyard (to the right), which was accessed from the harbour beneath the wooden planking. Today, this is part of the South West Coast Path. Across the harbour, a small GWR tank locomotive is seen at the head of a boat train made up of GWR clerestory coaches alongside the baggage hall. The Pavilion Theatre, which had recently opened in 1908, looks splendid.

Johnstone Row

The Johnstone estate, a glorious terrace from 1811, was named after Sir Frederic Johnstone, who had considerable property interests in the town. In this genteel late Victorian scene captured by the photographer, folk of all ages are making the best of a sunny morning. The first changes are being made to the Georgian terraces as businesses develop at ground-floor level. The dark-framed shopfront went on to become the Criterion restaurant, familiar to thousands of holidaymakers and locals for more than a century. The chairs on the sand are set up in front of what was known as the 'sea view concert platform, which was later occupied by Ballard Brown's troupe of entertainers.

The Tea Cabin and Horse-Drawn Cabs

The splendid Georgian terraces and Weymouth's two premier hotels, the Gloucester and the Royal, look down on an early afternoon scene. The horse-drawn coaches stand ready to transport their passengers to Upwey Wishing Well, Sutton Poyntz or Preston. A cluster of horse-drawn cabs are gathered in front of the Tea Cabin. The latter was opened in 1878 as a shelter for the cabmen as they waited for fares. The flag is flying above what was the American Studio, a photograph portraiture business, and carries the name 'Gee'. There were three photographers with the name Gee operating in Weymouth around this time.

The Sea View Concert Platform

The original Georgian bathing machines, with their distinctive octagonal roofs, are gathered in a group further along the sands. By this time, they were being replaced by the newer Victorian models with the pitched roof design. The latter appear to be acting as a protective wall to shelter the large audience captivated by a Pierrot show, possibly Catlin's Royal Pierrot troupe. As usual, some enterprising individuals have found a commanding position to view the late afternoon show. A few visitors have hollowed out small refuges in the sand to provide a more comfortable way of relaxing while enjoying the show.

St Thomas Street

In this bustling street scene, one or two shoppers have stopped to watch the cameraman, who is perhaps stood on a wagon to obtain the perfect shot. Outside Billet's dairy a horse waits patiently after bringing fresh milk or setting off with deliveries. This fascinating mixture of small businesses has sadly disappeared, but several of the features at first-floor level can still be seen, including the windows above the dairy and the buildings beyond No. 58. The first four properties to the right have not survived.

3   WEYMOUTH. – View from the Marine Hotel. — LL.

Alexandra Gardens Bandstand

The bandstand erected in 1891 dominates the Alexandra Gardens. The six ornate statues were donated by a former town mayor. Edwardian ladies relax in their deckchairs to enjoy the early afternoon sun as others stroll through the garden. At one time, the Corporation charged for entrance to the gardens and perhaps the two sentry-like booths by the gate were where the charges were paid. After much objection, the charges were removed in 1900. The bandstand was enclosed within a glass building known as the Kursaal. The thatched shelters were erected in 1904.

Afternoon Tea

The Marine Hotel, later renamed the Edward Hotel, has here been photographed from approximately where the booths are in the previous picture. The neighbouring Georgian terraces, Pulteney Buildings to the left and Bank Buildings to the right, overlook a scene of Edwardian gentility at its best. Afternoon tea is on offer as the Viennese Band serenades the strollers and those seated beneath their parasols. The contrast with today's lively atmosphere generated by the amusement arcade and various rides could not be greater. The absence of thatched shelters dates this image to before 1904. The Marine Hotel has since been converted to residential flats.

Aerial Views

The Nothe and Chapelhay

Photographers were quick to realise the pictorial and commercial opportunities presented by the emerging aviation industry. In this view from around 1919, the camera captures a wonderful view of Weymouth above the harbour and Melcombe Regis below. The early layout of the Alexandra Gardens is clear, while the Nothe and its barracks are clearly seen to the left of the vessel moored in the Cove. A paddle steamer is moored alongside Trinity Road. Holy Trinity church is seen in front of the town bridge and, above it, Holy Trinity School buildings dominate Chapelhay. The school and its surrounding buildings were destroyed during the air raids of 1940. The roof of St Mary's church dominates St Mary's Street with the Market Hall roof adjacent.

Portland Breakwater

After the two final sections of the Breakwater, seen here, were completed in 1905, Portland Harbour was finally enclosed, some 111 years after the idea was first proposed. This view was taken only two or three years later. Two GWR Channel Islands vessels are moored up in the Cove, while an unidentified sailing ship is alongside Trinity Road. The building with the large chimney is the Devenish brewery, and in the left-hand corner of the square are the twin oast chimneys of the John Groves brewery. Holy Trinity School is seen in the bottom-right corner.

The Esplanade and Park District

Melcombe Regis on a summer's morning in the mid-1920s. The houses and businesses of the Park District crowd the land to the rear of the Esplanade and its fine Georgian terraces. The bandstand on the promenade would shortly be removed and installed at the Nothe. In the bottom right of the picture, the rounded end of St John's mission hall can be seen in Chelmsford Street. While in King Street, the tower of Christchurch rises above Brunel's original overall railway station roof. The newly constructed Westham Bridge is visible in the top-right corner. The then recent extension of the promenade seawards from the Jubilee Clock is clearly seen.

The Sands

Visitors are taking full advantage of Weymouth's magnificent sands and the many entertainments and diversions available. The building just below Westham Bridge was at that time the Weymouth Engineering and Technical College, later to become the arts centre. The series of large curved roofs below the railway viaduct, formerly Betts Timber Yard, are now part of the car park between Commercial Road and Park Street. In the top right of the picture, reclamation work to form Radipole Park Drive and reclaim the land enclosed to extend the railway carriage sidings is well on the way to completion. The latter area is now a retail park.

The Pier Bandstand

An early morning view as the wave tops are caught by the breeze. The art deco-style Pier Bandstand dominates an area once known as the Narrows. It was at this point, during a storm known as the 'Great Gale' on the night of 23 November 1824, that the sea swept over the narrow spit, destroying the Esplanade and killing two men. At that time, the Backwater extended almost to the rear of the seafront terraces. Many familiar Weymouth landmarks, now long demolished or removed, can be seen. They include the gasworks, with the sun reflecting off the gas holder in Westwey Road, and the power station chimney in Stavordale Road. Also visible are the church towers of Gloucester Street Congregational and Christchurch, and to the right of the latter is the railway station roof.

The Park District and the Railway

Three Royal Navy vessels lie at anchor within the sheltered waters of Portland Harbour. The land seen in the bottom-right corner originally formed part of the Backwater and was reclaimed to be a pleasure park, but eventually provided housing and the land necessary for the expansion of the railway. This view, from the late 1940s, demonstrates just how important that industry was to Weymouth at that time, with the crowded sidings and size of the goods yard. Ranelagh Road lies to the left of the station with the houses of that area of the Park District; all the streets here were named after prominent Victorian Conservative statesmen, with the exception of Penny Street. The two taller buildings are St Augustine's School in Walpole Street and the Methodist church in Derby Street.

The Fire-Ravaged Ritz Theatre

Late summer 1954, and the skeletal steel framework of the Ritz theatre stands exposed to the elements following the fire that destroyed much of this beautiful wooden-clad building in April of that year. The magnificent glass conservatory and terrace of the Gloucester Hotel can be seen, and to its right is Weymouth's other premier hotel, the Royal. To the right of the railway viaduct a bank has been constructed prior to the back filling of the enclosed area to create the car park. The reed beds form the bulk of the Backwater, providing a haven for mosquitoes during much of my childhood. On the Westham bank, adjacent to the railway viaduct, stand the art deco shelters of the miniature railway, with the helter-skelter and other attractions of Chipperfield's funfair beyond.

Rodwell, Sandsfoot and Wyke

A mixture of old and new is seen in this 1960s panorama. To the north, the old borough of Melcombe stretches away past the Pier Bandstand towards Greenhill. The once busy railway line to Portland, now a scenic trailway, can be seen in the cutting as it passes under the bridge on Buxton Road. To its left is the Clearmount estate and to the right Rodwell Avenue. Both areas began to be developed in the mid-nineteenth century. Small sailing boats are moored in Sandsfoot Cove, a popular beach location for local folk. The new buildings of Chapelhay are prominent in the centre of the picture, replacing the many properties destroyed by enemy action in 1940. The Pavilion Theatre of 1960 dominates the entrance to the pier and quayside.

Sands and Beach

The aerial view and that on the following page were both taken on the same day in the 1950s. They show the magnificence of the sands and beach at Weymouth. The shallow waters, seen so clearly in this photograph, have always been an attractive and popular feature for those with families. Beyond the northern end of the Park District and St John's church, the larger buildings of Weymouth and District Hospital on Melcombe Avenue and the teacher training college alongside Dorchester Road stand out. In the distance, the Ridgeway looks down on open fields, which today are filled with the estates and houses lining Littlemoor Road.

The Pier Bandstand and Greenhill

The art deco Pier Bandstand was designed to resemble the great transatlantic liners of the 1930s and recreate the impression of being at sea. Today, all that remains is that part of the building beneath the black roof. A popular venue with a large open area in front of the stage, it was always at its best on a fine sunny day or a warm summer's evening. Below, the pontoon of the White Motor Boats is not open for business. Trips across the bay to view the ships of the Royal Navy in Portland Harbour were operated from this location and another, by Messrs Cosens, from a similar pontoon near the Jubilee Clock Tower. The rows of beach huts operated by the firm Damers and available for hire occupy the shingle beach from Brunswick Terrace towards Greenhill Gardens.

28

Greenhill & Lodmoor

Lodmoor and the Glidabout Boats
It is the 1930s, and judging from the large crowd gathered in rather formal dress it is perhaps the seasonal opening of the Glidabout boating lake at Lodmoor. This appears to have been located somewhere near to where the Sea Life centre is today. I am uncertain as to how the boats were powered; my research has only revealed that the Glidabout Company was based in Southend. The huts in the background are on the beach adjacent to the sea wall on Preston Road.

The Sluice Gardens

Another donation to the town by Sir Frederic Johnstone MP, the Sluice Gardens, also known as Spoon Gardens, were built on what was the main drain for Lodmoor. They were necessary, as much of the land is barely above sea level. The gardens were replaced by chalets and a paddling pool. Just beyond the garage building in the background is where the Glidabout boats operated, pictured on page 29. The white art deco house on the distant hill was a landmark for years, but was eventually surrounded by residential housing.

Greenhill Gardens

In 1902, the Greenhill Gardens were yet another gift to the town from Sir Frederic Johnstone (although the town's people had been allowed access since 1872). The Johnstones' ownership of the land had been contested, unsuccessfully, by Thomas Wallis, a councillor. The latter maintained that the site was common land. In this view from around 1906, we see the gardens after they were extended. The fencing around the tennis courts can be seen and there are boats on the shingle. It is not known if these were fishing boats or pleasure boats for hire.

The Bungalows and Chalets, Greenhill

It is the mid-1930s, and the photographer, who stands in front of the houses seen in the background of the picture at the top of this page, is looking south. In 1920, the chalets were constructed as a single-storey block with a small promenade on top. The second storey was added to the block in the background in 1933. The Greenhill Bowling Club, established in 1910, is above the chalets in the foreground. The blocks were to be demolished but Grade II listed status was given.

The Floral Clock, 1936

The splendid floral clock in Greenhill Garden also used a cuckoo call to mark the hour. It was built and installed in 1936 by the well-known clock maker James Ritchie & Son of Edinburgh, who still specialise in steeple and public clocks. Weymouth has been blessed with a number of attractive gardens and many of the flowers and shrubs were grown by the parks and gardens department in the greenhouses situated in Melcombe Gardens, adjacent to the swannery.

Coronation Year, 1953

The parks and gardens department excelled themselves once more in this year of celebration, when the image of the crown was to be found everywhere. This creation near to the floral clock in Greenhill Gardens was no exception. As the bleak post-war years ended, it was bright floral displays such as this that lifted the spirits and fostered a feeling of optimism. It is difficult to compare this attractive scene with the gory one following the Monmouth Rebellion, when a gallows was erected here to hang those local men convicted by Judge Jeffreys at the Bloody Assizes.

GREENHILL GARDENS, WEYMOUTH   8574

Refreshment Kiosk at Greenhill

The refreshment kiosk at Greenhill pictured sometime in the late 1940s. From the choppy nature of the sea and the fluttering tablecloths, we can assume that the offer for tea for 1s 2d will not attract many to sit outside. Today this would have the usual clutter of boards, flags and banners advertising various brands. The kiosk was replaced with the two-storey brick building we have today that offers a much wider range than the simple tariff available when this picture was taken.

Greenhill and the Pier Bandstand at Night

Greenhill Gardens on a calm summer's evening and individual flower beds and features are all illuminated, creating pools of bright colour. The fairy lights stretched the length of the promenade and the added effect of their reflection on the water, particularly at high water, created a fantastic atmosphere. The illuminated sweep of the bay was always impressive, particularly as you approached the town by the old road over the Ridgeway. One can only imagine the effect on a wartime population, so accustomed to blackout regulations, when these lights were first turned on. It must have been dramatic.

The Promenade

The Promenade at Greenhill
The photographer has set up his camera on a walkway on the two-storey chalet block at Greenhill. The Weymouth promenade runs southwards from the Sluice Gardens at Lodmoor for approximately 1½ miles. Here, in this view from the early 1920s, there are beach huts available for hire. This area was, and remains today, a favourite with local folk. The wooden beach huts with removable canvas sides are beginning to replace the earlier tented variety. The earlier formal hedgerows within Greenhill Gardens are being replaced with more informal shrubberies and flower beds.

The Burdon Bandstand

There were two attractive cast-iron bandstands on Weymouth seafront, the other being in the Alexandra Gardens. The bandstand pictured here was erected in 1907. Crowds listening to the performance frequently resulted in bottlenecks, and in 1920 the promenade was widened to alleviate the problem. The bandstand disappeared in the late 1930s when the Pier Bandstand was constructed. The photograph was probably taken in midweek, as there appear to be few men among those strolling or listening to the band.

The Pier Bandstand

Photographed shortly after it opened in May 1939, the Pier Bandstand was initially subject to much criticism (particularly as to how it intruded into the sweep of the bay). It remains a matter for discussion today, even though the pier portion was removed in 1986. The open deck area and stage were supported on angled concrete piles, producing a ramshackle appearance in contrast to the art deco design of the upper structures. This card was posted in December 1939 and the sender of the card is being less than discreet; her message gives details of her two sons and their individual military postings.

Harry Hudson and His Showband

Opening in early summer 1939, it was sadly a very short season for the Pier Bandstand with the outbreak of war. However, normal service was resumed after the war and entertainment returned. Harry Parry, a band leader popular on the BBC's *Radio Rhythm Club*, appeared for a few seasons. He was followed by Harry Hudson, seen here in 1958, with his showband, who appeared for a number of seasons. A proportion of the musicians would have been local. Harry Hudson was also the pianist on the BBC's audience participation radio show *Have a Go*, hosted by Wilfred Pickles. Hudson actually took over when Violet Carson (Ena Sharples of *Coronation Street* fame) left. Other popular events at the pier were dances, talent shows, a bathing beauty contest and Dale Martin's professional wrestling.

Boats for Hire

This area of the beach was occupied by the four concessions seen. Each offered facilities for bathers to change in the cubicles provided for a small charge; they were the successors to the Georgian and Victorian bathing machines. One could also hire small clinker-built rowing boats or canoes, usually by the hour or half hour. Edgar Wallis was a former Weymouth mayor, councillor and hotelier for many years. The pontoon visible below the Pier Bandstand was operated by the White Motor Boat company and offered motor boat trips across the bay to Portland Harbour to view the Royal Navy's warships.

The Promenade from a Window on Brunswick Terrace
The motor car is beginning to make its presence felt in this scene of busy summer activity from around 1950. Although parking remained unrestricted, there were locations where a charge was made for supervised parking. The two gentlemen with white armbands were the attendants at this location. The other gent, in the gaiters, is an AA patrolman who, with his motorcycle and sidecar full of tools, could be found here. A member of the AA, identified by the badge attached to the radiator grille or bumper, would receive a smart salute of acknowledgement.

The Promenade Opposite Royal Crescent
The gent in the white trousers and his companion are making the best of the morning's sunshine around 1895. The Victorian shelter would most probably have been removed when the promenade in front of the Jubilee Clock was extended and the road was widened, swallowing up this part of the promenade. Fortunately, many of the shelters have survived, despite being exposed to the worst of the weather. The gap created when the former Stacie's Hotel was demolished can be seen beyond the King Street junction.

The Jubilee Clock

A landmark on the promenade for generations, the Jubilee Clock Tower was erected to celebrate the Golden Jubilee of Queen Victoria and unveiled on 31 October 1888. The funds from a public subscription paid for the tower and Sir Henry Edwards gifted the clock. The tower is 44 feet high and each clock face is 4 feet 8 inches in diameter. It stands today in exactly the same position shown in this view. The promenade was extended and the road widened in the 1920s. The billboard is advertising a concert of military and orchestral music at the bandstand in the Alexandra Gardens.

Promenade and Fairy Lights

A summer's afternoon and the striking difference between then and now is the formal dress of those enjoying the fine weather. The ladies are all in long dresses and parasols, the gentlemen are suited and wearing hats. Between the flagpoles, small glass jars containing candles are suspended. These would be lowered each summer evening and the candles lit to provide illumination. The promenade now extends forward from this shelter. To the left is Royal Terrace, and the building at the junction with King Street was demolished to allow buses and large vehicles to negotiate the turn.

The New Promenade Extension

A few years have passed since the picture above was taken, and dramatic changes are apparent. Neither the Jubilee Clock nor the Victorian shelter have moved, the promenade has been extended and more space has been created. The other purpose of the extension was to prevent the shingle beach encroaching onto the sands. The road has been widened by absorbing the part of the promenade that was to the left of the clock in the picture above. The Tett family opened their confectionery business in 1901 and by the time of this photograph had added the restaurant advertised on the wall.

A Crowded Promenade

A few of the original Georgian bathing machines are still in use in this view from around 1919. However, the problem of a very crowded promenade on busy summer days, as seen in the picture above, was becoming more urgent. Movement would certainly have been restricted, and the photographer has attracted a lot of attention from his elevated position. The extension work described on the previous page was undertaken around the Jubilee Clock, and in the following years extensions were made to the promenade southwards towards King's Statue, including this section.

An Extended Promenade

In this photograph from around 1930, the widening work has been completed and a much more comfortable experience is provided for strollers. The small, white pillars with chains were shortly to be removed, but one remains as a memorial to the Great Gale of November 1824, which destroyed part of the promenade. The advertisement for Tett's restaurant has been joined by others extolling the virtues of Gilbey's Invalid Port and Watney's Ales. Sales of Gilbey's Invalid Port, marketed at that time as a tonic, were responsible for enabling the company to revive its financial fortunes.

The Tea Cabin
The octagonal Tea Cabin opened in 1878 as the Cabmen's Shelter, providing refreshments for the drivers of the horse-drawn carriages that gathered in the area around King's Statue. Since that time, it has survived the reign of six monarchs, millions of customers, the First World War and the Second World War, during which it managed to remain open despite the sands being barred to visitors by barricades and barbed wire. On the sands the Georgian bathing machines have been joined by two larger bathing saloons.

Taxis for Hire
The internal combustion engine has displaced the horse-drawn cab, although pleasure trips were still available with horse power. A fine collection of taxi cabs awaits customers while their drivers are probably enjoying a cuppa in the Tea Cabin. The extent of the widening and extensions to the promenade are also clearly visible. The Georgian bathing machines have disappeared and the larger saloons have been joined by a number of individual chalets to preserve the modesty of bathers.

Esplanade, Weymouth.

J. W. Broomfield, Stationer, Weymouth.

The View from York Terrace

The promenade, viewed from York Terrace in the early 1890s. The large gap to the right of the Gloucester Hotel is where Stacie's Hotel once stood. There appears to be no building activity on the site and it was to remain that way until 1896. The large shrubs in the wooden tubs were a feature of the seafront at that time. The bathing saloons have extended into the shallow waters and it is this latter feature of the waters that has popularised Weymouth as a resort for families. Broomfields, who commissioned this card, also had a butchers and poultry shop in King Street.

The Esplanade, Weymouth.

S. 1602

Vintage Motor Cars

Nearly forty years have passed and much has changed in this view from the same location. The Royal Hotel occupies the gap seen in the previous picture. The gentleman in the road is a car park attendant.

The Southern Promenade
In this view from the mid-1930s, the photographer is standing in approximately the same position as in the previous photograph. Already, the motor car is beginning to have an impact. The large white stage on the sands is hosting the Val Vaux troupe of entertainers. In the distance, the Skee Ball pavilion can be seen, and beyond it is the Ritz theatre dominating the entrance to the pier. The Alexandra Gardens Theatre can just be seen at the top right.

The Sand Artist
The statue of Sir Henry Edwards, former MP for the town and its most generous benefactor, surveys the promenade from his plinth. An enterprising individual has taken the opportunity of low water to use the sands and the stone groyne as his easel, presenting a range of illustrations for strollers. The bandstand in the Alexandra Gardens dates this view to around 1910. Almost all the ground we see in this picture has been reclaimed from the sea. The land where the gardens previously stood was known as the Rings. The Nothe is in the background with part of the old barracks visible on the skyline.

The Beach & Sands

3544 Weymouth. Beach, looking West.

Where Sand and Shingle Meet
Both the views on this and the opposite page are from around 1890 and were published by Jeffery's, a stationer, bookseller and wool retailer, of No. 98 St Mary Street. In later years, they also operated a printing business. Distinct from albumen prints, they are both photographic prints of interest, as are the legends describing the scene, which is perhaps an early form of the postcard view. As it does today, the Jubilee Clock marks the point where the sands and shingle beach meet. In the view above it is clear that shingle encroachment onto the sands was already a problem.

3542 Weymouth, Esplanade, looking East

The View from the Alexandra Gardens

The former Stacie's Hotel, with its impressive bow windows, can be seen in both photographs. In the lower view, it is low water and it would appear that a considerable amount of seaweed has been left by the falling tide. Presumably the horse is enjoying the therapeutic qualities of the water before towing the individual bathing machines and their clients into the sea to share that benefit. In various early views from my collection, young men with baskets can be seen, presumably offering various items for sale.

'The Narrows'

Scenes of perfect relaxation take place as folk enjoy the sea air from tents and deck chairs, perhaps contemplating a short trip in rowing boat. Imagine, then, the scene almost a hundred years earlier in the Great Gale of 23 November 1924. The sea swept across this part of the beach, known then as 'The Narrows'. It was only this narrow spit of land that separated the sea from the Backwater. Two men were killed as they tried to cross during the storm. The man with the horse and cart is intriguing. Is he clearing seaweed or offering goods for sale? Among those offering boats for hire is Kelly's, who continued to operate well into the 1960s.

Boats for Hire

Some forty years after the previous view and the beach scene has changed only slightly. People are still enjoying themselves but the commercial activity has increased. There are three or four concessions offering boats and canoes for hire. This includes Kelly's, which at this time was operated by the Bugler family. For the more modest, there are huts available offering private changing facilities. To the right at the water's edge are floats, which consisted of two hulls linked by three panels with the centre panel acting as a seat. A double-bladed paddle was used for propulsion.

A Paddling Paradise
The camera has caught the attention of several youngsters in this photograph from around 1910. There are two beach vendors with their white coats and aprons. The problem of shingle encroachment on to the sands is once more very apparent, and it was to be another twenty years before work was undertaken to extend the promenade beyond the Jubilee Clock to the area in the foreground of this view. Several other shoreline projects have been implemented over the years to lessen the effect of the prevailing current that carries the shingle. It is to be hoped that Weymouth's finest asset, it sands, will be protected.

Sand Castles and Bathing Machines
The photographer has gone unnoticed as he takes this picture; the digging of holes and the building of sandcastles is the priority for the young, while the adults enjoy the sunshine and sea air from a deckchair or take a stroll. The bathing machines have been taken to the water for their occupants to descend gracefully for a swim while maintaining their modesty. The only alterations in today's scene are the absence of bathing machines and the addition of railings along the promenade edge.

Summer Crowds

The height of summer and the sands are crowded with holidaymakers anxious to take advantage of the sunshine; perhaps the presence of so many jackets suggests that the temperature was not so high. However, every opportunity to enjoy the sun was taken, even if the long hours spent exposed would usually require a generous application of Calamine lotion to ease the discomfort of the inevitable sunburn. The chalet with the vertical stripes was one of many along the sands that sold ice creams, candyfloss and other refreshments. Each evening, these chalets would receive the attention of local youngsters, who, armed with a variety of impromptu sieving devices, would hunt for small change dropped into the sand during the day.

The Punch and Judy Man

A mid-morning entertainment has attracted a large audience while the Punch and Judy booth has been delivered by wheelbarrow. I wonder if those gents stood just to the left are the operators. The authorities did not seem to worry about clearing the seaweed from the shoreline. In the heat of the day, it would certainly have attracted flies and other insects, apart from emitting an unpleasant smell. The large bathing saloons have been drawn out into the water and a few of the original Georgian bathing machines are still in use in this view from the early 1900s.

An Artist in Sand

Sand artist is the description, and who could argue with that? Jack Hayward is seen at work on one of the many fine cathedral models he created using only sand and seawater. Jack worked on these sculptures in the years following the Second World War. In the picture above, the hand pump used to keep the sand moist can be seen in the bucket. These beautifully crafted and detailed models never failed to draw a crowd, who would show their appreciation by tossing coins into a bucket with a canvas cover and a slot. Jack was succeeded by Fred Darrington in the early 1950s. Fred created many different models and displays and introduced colour.

Entertainments on the Sands

As the popularity of the seaside holiday grew dramatically between the two World Wars, the demand for entertainment and activities also increased. In this view, when the delights of digging a very large hole in the sand had lost its attraction, a child could pester for a donkey or goat ride, a ride on a carousel or a slide down the helter-skelter. The large white building in the background offered the diversion of a vaudeville show. The Dorothy restaurant advertisement painted on the wall to the left of the helter-skelter can still be seen today.

Pierrot Shows

Pierrot shows were a popular open-air entertainment on the beaches of many resorts and Weymouth was no exception. Pierrots appeared around the 1890s as the novelty and popularity of the blackface minstrels began to wane. Some Pierrots performed with whitened faces, using a mixture of zinc and lard. Unlike the Minstrel shows, Pierrots offered a variety of entertainment. Will Catlin, whose real name was William Fox, was known as the 'King of the Pierrots'. Starting in 1894, he eventually ran a number of troupes in several seaside resorts, including Weymouth. Catlin favoured all male troupes who were immaculately turned out in the traditional baggy white suits, black pompoms and conical hats. Mr Catlin's great-granddaughter told me that he used 'royal' in their title after performing for King George V.

Seaside Vaudeville

The Val Vaux vaudesque troupe, seen in this photograph, continued the tradition of entertaining visitors between the two World Wars. The company, now including men and women, still retained some elements of the white, baggy suits, including pompoms and frilly collars. The shows were presented from a purpose-built stage on the sands in front of Chesterfield Place. Val Vaux's real name was William Valentine Whitehouse-Vaux and he is seen standing to the far right behind his wife, whose stage name was Ruby Lee. The final season for the vaudesques was in 1939, and sadly this traditional style of open-air entertainment did not return with peace. Others who provided entertainment were the members of Mr Ballard Brown's group, who operated from a location on the sands opposite the King's Statue.

The Esplanade & Terraces

3759. ESPLANADE & PAVILION, WEYMOUTH.

Pulteney and Devonshire Buildings
The southernmost of all the seafront terraces are the Devonshire and Pulteney Buildings, seen in this view beyond the Skee Ball pavilion. Skee Ball was a variation of skittles that crossed the Atlantic. The greater part of the land in this view had been reclaimed from the sea on the suggestion of Sir William Pulteney. The construction of the two terraces began in 1812 and continued for seven years. Pulteney had changed his name from Johnstone upon marrying into the wealthy Bath family of Pulteneys. It is pleasing to note that these two terraces remain virtually as built, although the exterior colour schemes would perhaps draw comments from the original builders.

Clarence Buildings

The tall building behind the statue of Sir Frederic Johnstone, now the Rex Hotel, was built in the first decade of Queen Victoria's reign. The building to the right in the picture is on the corner of St Alban Street, and was a forerunner of the Georgian architecture seen elsewhere on the seafront. Originally a two-storey building, a third storey was later added. The entrance, originally in St Alban Street, was later removed, presumably when it was amalgamated with the adjoining building (now also a hotel). Sir Henry Edwards was a wealthy Weymouth born man, who was one of two MPs for the town. He was a generous man and gifted much to the town.

Augusta Place

It is in this area of Melcombe Regis that the first properties were 'turned' to face the sea as the fashionable practice of 'taking the waters' increased. An embankment was constructed and the former practice of using the sands as a rubbish dump ceased. Eventually, the promenade was constructed. The varied early Georgian design of individual buildings is in contrast to the later terraces, where properties shared features and design. The covered porch of the Victoria Hotel, formerly Luce's Hotel, can be seen.

Charlotte Row

The building built in 1795 with the Ionic columns and balcony was Harvey's library, card and assembly rooms in Weymouth's Georgian heyday. When this photograph was taken, it was most probably the Royal Dorset Yacht Club, hosting crews from racing yachts, including Sir Tommy Lipton. To the right are the York Buildings from the eighteenth century. Set back are the long-demolished buildings of Chesterfield Place. It is here that the blockhouse gun emplacement was located in the seventeenth century. Beyond is Johnstone Row, developed around 1811. Fortunately, the first property in the row, including the original bow front, entrance and stone steps, has survived.

Royal Terrace

The building of Royal Terrace commenced around 1815 and occupied what was once known as the Royal Shrubbery, which had been laid out by George's brother, the Duke of Gloucester. It seems that the erection of the King's Statue, seen just beyond the man with the wheelbarrow, was a spur to the building of this Georgian terrace and many others. The elegance of their original condition equalled any of those to be found in Bath. Royal Terrace today, at ground level, is an ugly sprawl of mismatched modern shopfronts and bus shelters.

The King's Statue

Arguably the man responsible for the advent of the seaside holiday, King George III has dominated Weymouth for nearly 200 years. When it was first erected, the statue of 'farmer George', as he was affectionately known, looked out over a rather unattractive piece of ground to his left. The statue is constructed from Coade stone, and it is a tribute to the quality of the material that His Majesty has retained his appearance, and thus his dignity, despite being so exposed to the abrasive effects of wind, sand and sea for so long. Coade stone was also valued for the quality of detail that could be achieved.

Gloucester Row

William Henry, Duke of Gloucester, was the younger brother of George III and decided to build Gloucester Lodge, the second building from the left with the Venetian style windows flanking the conservatory. He believed that his health would benefit from exposure to the sea air. The larger four-storey building to the left was added in 1860 on land known as 'the Shrubbery'. It was to the original two-storey building that George III came for his first visit in 1789. His visits continued almost annually until 1805. The King would cross a track and climb into the royal saloon before it was pulled into the sea. As His Royal Highness emerged from the saloon into the water, a group of musicians would play the National Anthem.

The Royal Hotel

The Royal Hotel is pictured here in 1899, two years after it opened (replacing Stacie's Hotel, which had previously stood at this location). There was a delay in building the new hotel when the expected investment failed to materialise. However, it stands as a tribute to its Victorian designers and the many craftsmen involved in its construction. Eric Ricketts, author of *The Buildings of Old Weymouth*, describes the building as having 'just that touch of opulence required to season the austere dignity of the earlier terraces'. To the left is the fourth of the buildings by Hamilton that adjoined Gloucester Lodge, with its distinctive Georgian proportions and embellishments. Beyond, on the right, two Georgian buildings were demolished and replaced with the Royal Arcade and two shops. Today, only one shop remains – Rossi's Ice Cream Parlour.

Royal Crescent

The building of Royal Crescent commenced around 1795, and the original intention was to construct forty-nine houses on a slight crescent. However, fifteen were completed and a short road linking to Crescent Street at the rear was built. If completed as originally designed, this would have been a magnificent sight occupying the next two terraces visible in this view. It could possibly have rivalled its Bath namesake. The adjoining Belvedere Terrace was begun in 1818 and is another terrace with some very attractive features. The large flag advertises the Savoy Café. In the 1920s, Weymouth council prevented any further retail development within these terraces, so we enjoy them today in their (almost) original condition.

Victoria Terrace

An open-top omnibus emerges onto the Esplanade to join an interesting selection of vehicles, both motorised and man-powered. The advertisement at the front of the bus is for Dominey's, the butcher's of St Mary Street. The construction of Victoria Terrace, to the left, commenced in 1855 and its scale and design is sympathetic to its neighbours, both north and south. The Burdon Hotel, now the Prince Regent, dominates, but a balance is achieved with the adjoining buildings. Sandringham, the building with the portico nearest the camera, was at one point occupied by the YWCA.

Waterloo Place

The construction of Waterloo Place commenced in 1835, some twenty years after Wellington's great victory, when public pride in that victory remained. The similarity of design to the Devonshire, Pulteney and Brunswick terraces is striking. Fortunately, only a couple of the original two-storey bow windows have been lost and once more the sympathetic exterior decoration imposed by the local authority only adds to its attraction today. The other striking feature is the wonderful collection of chimney pots. St John's School can be seen at the junction with William Street.

Brunswick Terrace

Building Brunswick Terrace (originally built as Brunswick Buildings) was a brave venture in 1828, particularly as it was only four years earlier that the Great Gale of 1824 had swept across this area of the seafront. It remains one of the more exposed terraces to the sea and weather. Perhaps this exposure was the reason for the doors being blocked off in the bow-fronted end of the terrace? A family member who occupied a part of the property above the doorway can attest to it being a particularly draughty location. The rounded end of the terrace creates a pleasing architectural link with others on the seafront.

The Harbour

The Rubble Pier

The buildings to the left and the pier visible in this picture are all on land reclaimed from the sea. Because of its original coarse construction, the pier was known as the 'rubble pier'. The building work in progress in this late 1880s view was most probably for the baggage warehouse, customs offices and the extension of the quay tramway for the Channel Islands services (completed in 1889). The public were also able to walk on the pier to a point just out of view in this picture. The cannon is from the Crimean War. The town council acquired the gun from the government and it was positioned here after initially being displayed in front of Pulteney Buildings.

NERAL VIEW. WEYMOUTH.

The Wooden Pier

The baggage warehouse, offices and pier improvements are now complete. Alongside the quay is a GWR steamer from the Channel Islands passenger service – it could be either *The Roebuck* or *The Reindeer*. An unidentified paddle steamer from the Cosens fleet is also awaiting passengers. Cosens operated an extensive service along this part of the South Coast, visiting local attractions and towns. The improvements and additions to the promenade are also seen, but the Crimea cannon has disappeared.

Pier Improvements

Further improvements to the old wooden pier were required due to increasing business to the Channel Islands together with the demands of the tourist trade. In 1931, major works were begun and a reinforced concrete pier was constructed. The work was completed and the pier opened in 1933. It was extended by another 300 feet, with the addition of a promenade, shelters, changing facilities for bathers and a diving stage. The viewing platforms above the changing rooms provided visitors an ideal place to view the cranes unloading or loading. A 1930s train of GWR passenger stock awaits passengers alongside the quay platform.

The Stone Pier

To the left is the wooden or Pleasure Pier, with two Channel Islands vessels alongside the quay. The Stone Pier, to the right, was originally a short stone jetty that was severely damaged in the storm of November 1824. An extension of 250 feet, intended to act as a breakwater for the protection of ships and the pier opposite, was added in 1876. In recent years, storms battered the pier and reinforcement works were completed in the 1980s. Further into the harbour, several other cargo ships are moored to the quay at the rear of Devonshire and Pulteney Buildings.

The New Alongside the Old

An interesting view of the harbour from the early 1960s depicts the old fleet of Channel Islands vessels preparing to give way to newer ships. *Caeserea*, dominating the photograph, was completed at Samuel White's shipyard on the Isle of Wight with her sister ship *Sarnia*. They were the final passenger ferries to be built for the Channel Islands services. They were also the last conventional, non-high-speed ferries of any type to be built for that market for thirty-eight years. Both vessels were capable of carrying 1,400 passengers. Caesearea and Sarnia were the respective roman names for Jersey and Guernsey. Across the harbour, a Cosens paddle steamer is on the slipway for service.

Four mast schooner. "YXPILA . RAUMA at Weymouth from Finland. Timber cargo.

Timber from Finland

The magnificent four-mast schooner *Yxpila*, from Rauma in Finland, was a regular visitor to Weymouth Harbour and has understandably attracted a crowd of admirers. As can be seen in the photograph, her cargo was timber. One horse-drawn wagon is being loaded while another waits, perhaps to be transported to Betts Timber Yard along Commercial Road. The tracks of the harbour tramway can also be seen. The building with the three storeys of bay windows is today No. 12 Custom House Quay, although the ground-floor windows have been removed.

Harbour Entrance

Weymouth Harbour entrance and a couple of small craft are on the move. To the left is the Nothe, with the footpath that leads to the Stone Pier, and beyond the trees is the slipway. Further on are the closely packed buildings of the harbour side and Chapelhay. A Channel Islands cargo vessel is alongside the Wooden Pier and the four cranes dominate the skyline of the harbour. Their operations were a constant source of interest to local folk and visitors as they unloaded or loaded ships moored alongside.

Ferry Steps

The ferrymen are busy conveying passengers across the harbour. This was always a popular service and another boat is just approaching, while another takes a break. The ferry service still operates today. Across the harbour, old and new rub shoulders. The *Yxpila Rauma*, a magnificent four-mast schooner, is seen across the harbour. The ship to the right is a freighter from the GWR Channel Islands fleet. The booms to the left are part of a slipway used for boat repairs.

The Cove

The Cove is providing sheltered mooring for two unidentified GWR Channel Islands vessels and three smaller vessels; the latter are perhaps tugs from the Cosens fleet. The houses of Cove Row, with their interesting selection of architectural styles, are overlooked by the former home of the cavalry, the Red Barracks. That building has been redeveloped as houses and flats. The chimney and large building to its right were part of Groves' brewery.

OLD TOWN BRIDGE, WEYMOUTH.

The Town Bridge of 1824

This bridge, seen above, was the first to be built of stone. All previous bridges, the first constructed in the 1590s, were wooden. Further work was carried out in 1880 and a new swing section, seen here, was installed. A toll was imposed to pay for the work, although tolls were removed in 1889. The bridge was demolished, prior to replacement, in 1928, as was the building behind the bridge with the bow-fronted windows. This building also had shops at street level.

Royal Opening of the New Town Bridge

It is 4 July 1930 and the new bridge has just been officially opened by HRH the Duke of Kent, later to become George VI, in the naval dress uniform. He is talking to the town's mayor, Mr Percy Boyle. The gentleman in the gown and wig is the town clerk, Percy Smallman. The Lord Lieutenant for Dorset, Anthony Ashley-Cooper (7th Earl of Shaftesbury), is standing to the right of the mayor and to his rear is the town mace bearer. Immediately after the opening, the Cosens paddle steamer *Empress* passed through the raised bridge carrying local schoolchildren.

The New Town Bridge

The New Town Bridge proudly displays its hydraulically operated double-leaf bascules. The design gave an increase in width, thus allowing larger vessels access to the inner harbour. The paddle steamers of Cosens' fleet benefitted from that increased width as they were able to pass through and moor alongside the company workshop. The building to the left was the Palladium cinema, which occupied the former premises of Hawkes, Freeman hardware shop. The cinema closed in 1931 and during the Second World War became a club for armed services personnel. At the end of the war, Pankhurst's motorcycle showrooms took over the premises.

The Harbour from Town Bridge, Weymouth

North Quay

The inner harbour and North Quay in the early 1950s. Today, this area is much changed; all the buildings to the left along North Quay have been demolished, including Tudor House, believed to have been the harbourmaster's house, which is visible just behind the parked vehicles with its distinctive stone gable end. The final building to go was the fire station, and the training tower is seen rising above the roof line. Sidney Hall and Weymouth football ground, the latter known to generations as 'the Rec', have been replaced with a Supermarket.

The View from Chapelhay in the 1920s

A barge is being towed past Ferry's Corner in this view over the rooftops of Chapelhay. On the shoreline to the left, along what is today Westwey Road, several boats have been beached. The wooden Westham Bridge, opened in 1859, can be seen with the Backwater dam just in front. The latter was constructed in 1872 in an attempt to control tidal flows and to maintain water levels upriver, neither of which was ever achieved satisfactorily. The sharpness of the curve on Ferry's Corner, where the paddle steamer is moored, proved problematic for the railway and improvements were carried out as infilling took place. Today this area of the harbour is filled with the pontoons and boats of the Marina.

The Swannery & Radipole Lake

The Swans
The photographer has attracted the attention of the swans, who are hoping to be fed. This view, taken from the junction of King Street and Commercial Road, is dominated by the (then) lengthy wooden trestles of Westham Bridge. It is clear just how much of the Backwater was to be reclaimed. On the high ground in the distance are the buildings of Chapelhay and the northern end of Wyke Regis. The larger of the two chimneys is that of the electricity power station in Stavordale Road, completed in 1904, a few months before this photograph was taken. The smaller tower is part of the gasworks.

Wooden Railway Viaduct

This view is from almost the same location as the previous page but looking to the north. The wooden trestle bridge carries the railway to Portland via Rodwell and Wyke Regis. Trains from Weymouth station to Portland would run north from the station, clear the junction and then run south onto the bridge. In 1909, Melcombe Regis station was built as part of construction of a new bridge and viaduct to remove this time-consuming manoeuvre. The new steel girder bridge was built alongside the trestle bridge and the latter was then removed. The reclamation of the land by infilling between the new viaduct and Commercial Road was to follow. In the distance, the high ground at the end of Cassiobury Road is also known as Black Rock.

The New Westham Bridge
The construction of what would be renamed Westham Bridge is nearing completion in this view from around 1920. To be precise, it is a dam rather than a bridge, with eight culverts allowing the water to flow from the River Wey into the harbour and to the sea. Considerable land reclamation was required for its construction and further reclamation was to take place to the right of the picture and to the left on the opposite bank. The temporary wooden bridge used during construction can also be seen. To the right, the brick railway viaduct is just visible.

The Bowling Green and Tennis Courts
The reclamation work has been completed and the land used to provide space for recreation and relaxation. The bowling green, tennis courts and pleasure gardens were put to good use from the mid-1920s until the 1970s, when they disappeared under tarmac to provide car parking. The curved roof, with the tower of Christchurch behind, was the corner of Betts Timber Yard on Commercial Road, now another car park. The larger of the two buildings on the skyline is the Convent of the Sacred Heart on Carlton Road.

The Boating Lake

In addition to reclaiming land for the benefit of the community, the area that had been known as the Backwater was renamed Radipole Lake and became an asset for leisure use. The ever-hungry swans remain as popular as always with holidaymakers. Other folk queue for the opportunity to take a boat onto the water. Further reclamation of land beneath and beyond the railway viaduct would commence in the early 1950s to provide more car parking space. The greenhouses from which the parks department provided many of the flowers for the town's public gardens can be seen top right.

Radipole Park Drive Gardens

The proposed development of the Royal Victoria Park never came to be, as the land was used for housing and became the Park District. However, the original plan included a western esplanade, also known as Western Walk, and this was built from King Street to Alexander Bridge at Hanover Road. It was lost in the 1920s when infilling to provide railway sidings and Radipole Park Drive was begun. However, in 1933, a plan was launched to extend the development that had begun with the Melcombe Regis Gardens northwards. It stretched alongside Radipole Lake and provided more tennis courts, a playing field and paddling pool. There were more plans to extend the infilling into the lake and provide more attractions, but the Second World War brought these plans to a halt. Despite this, Radipole Gardens, as seen here, were built.

The River Wey

The cycle ride to this location must have been a challenge, given the apparent condition of the road surface. It is here that the River Wey enters Radipole Lake and it is believed that the Romans may have established a port, as it was probably navigable to this point at that time. Considerable evidence of Roman activity at this end of the lake has been discovered to support this theory. Some indications of prehistoric activity have also been found. Radipole is an unusual place name, the origins of which are still uncertain.

Radipole Lake

At the time this photograph was taken, the lake would have been tidal. The construction of Westham Bridge with the sluice mechanisms has prevented this and today the lake is freshwater and a wonderful wildlife habitat has been created. A spring was discovered in the locality during the 1830s with sulphuretted hydrogen content and a spa was established and frequented by visitors until 1875.

The Nothe & Sandsfoot

The Nothe

The Nothe headland dominates the entrance to Weymouth Harbour and through the centuries was the obvious position to mount defensive positions to protect the port and town. The construction of the fort, prominent in this view, commenced in 1860 and was completed twelve years later. Along with other forms of defence along the South Coast, it was built to counter the perceived threat from France as the latter expanded their naval power. It played an active role in both World Wars and, following its purchase by the borough council, the local civic society undertook its restoration. It is now a popular visitor attraction.

The Nothe Gardens and Bandstand

It was 1889 when the Nothe Gardens were first planted formally. The path visible here is the Jubilee Walk, constructed to celebrate Queen Victoria's Jubilee, which follows the perimeter of the Nothe. The land adjacent to Nothe Fort was also used by the military for summer camps by the various yeomanry units, of which there are pictures in another chapter. As can be seen in this picture, the gardens provided a magnificent location for a view of the warships from the Channel Fleet anchored in Weymouth Bay or Portland Harbour.

Newton's Cove

In this view of Newton's Cove we can see the houses on the skyline that were occupied by the military at Nothe Fort. In the 1890s, the GWR planned to build a port here. The plan came to nothing but was not abandoned until 1913, so a pub, the Railway Dock Hotel, was built in anticipation. The white building with the conical black roof is possibly one of the original Georgian bathing machines rescued and used as a garden chalet.

The Underbarn

The Underbarn Walk seen in this view follows the coast edge from the Nothe to Sandsfoot Castle, the latter seen on the promontory in the distance. The cliffs are soft and have, over the centuries, been prone to landslips as the sea eats away at the base. One can only presume that without the erection of the Portland Harbour Breakwater, these cliffs would have been exposed to the full force of the wind and tide more frequently and suffered more serious erosion. The path is now closed to public access due to unstable ground conditions.

Sandsfoot Castle

Hostility with France was the recurring theme of the Middle Ages; following Henry VIII's split from the Church of Rome, the relationship with Catholic Europe did not improve. The threat of war was increased, and to protect the South Coast of England, Henry commenced the building of forts and castles. Sandsfoot, one such example, was designed to protect shipping in Portland Road (the area now enclosed within the Breakwater). Another was built on the Isle of Portland. It is believed that the stone was brought from one of the many abbeys the King destroyed, possibly Bindon Abbey near Wool. In this view from the Léon & Lévy collection, it is obvious that graffiti was a problem in the early 1900s.

The View from Castle Cove

Sandsfoot Castle was built in 1539 and, at that time, was in the middle of a field some distance from the cliff edge. Since then, as can be seen in this picture, erosion by the sea has left the castle in a very precarious position at the cliff edge. History does not tell us if the fort's guns were ever used, so it would appear that the deterrence factor was effective. The large building on the skyline is one of the buildings erected on Portland Breakwater.

Sandsfoot Tennis Lawn
The Isle of Portland dominates the horizon. The important strategic defensive position of Sandsfoot and its companion across the water on the isle are clear in this view from around the 1920s. Henry VIII was known to have a fondness for the game of real tennis, the forerunner of the modern game, so we can only assume he would have approved of the conversion of the castle lawns for tennis. The grounds have been converted to gardens in more recent years.

Castle Cove
Below the castle, Sandsfoot, or Castle Cove, became a popular location with the population of Wyke Regis as the area grew in the period between the wars and later on. It was always a popular spot for evening barbecues. The effects of erosion on the cliffs behind the beach are clear, and at the time of writing the Underbarn Path to the cove from the Nothe remains closed due to landslips. Today, Castle Cove is home to a thriving sailing club.

The Town Centre

Hurdles Corner

A picturesque view of Old Melcombe would be the more accurate description of this building, known to generations of Weymouth folk as 'Hurdles Corner'. Mr Hurdle opened his shop in the mid-nineteenth century, offering a wide range of foods and, as can be seen from the window display, an equally interesting choice of alcoholic drinks. The poster for the Pavilion is advertising 'Mother Goose', so we may assume the photograph was taken in the run up to Christmas. Sadly, these wonderful old buildings were demolished in the 1920s. Hurdles reopened in new premises on the site and traded until the 1980s.

St Mary's Street

We have come around the corner from the previous view and are looking north along St Mary's Street. Free admission was on offer to view 'Zena – the Magic Dot' in the premises of Joy Town, we can only speculate as to what that particular attraction may have been. Gosden's, whose sign dominates, also supplied the military and naval authorities. His business may well have extended into Maiden Street at the rear. Beyond St Mary's church is the market house; the latter was built and opened in the mid-1850s. The market in Melcombe dates back to 1280 and was held on a Tuesday, with an additional market on Monday granted when the charter was confirmed in 1318. The market hall was demolished in 1939.

The View from Bond Street

Photographed in the mid-1930s, we view St Mary's Street looking north from the junction with Upper Bond Street. The Woolworths store seen here opened in 1923 and, following the purchase of the adjoining building with the large advert for Halletts, an enlarged store was opened in 1938. The blind carries the legendary '3d and 6d stores'. To the left is V. H. Bennett's business, Weymouth's first department store. Opposite is Lovell's creamery, with an early milk float, complete with churn, ready to commence deliveries.

St Thomas Street

In this view of St Thomas Street, Weymouth's other main shopping street from the early years of the twentieth century, the splendour of the town's later Georgian architecture is shown at its best. Sadly, many of the buildings to the left (west) side of the street have been replaced. Opposite, on the east side, much of what can be seen at the first floor levels and above remains today. This area has now been pedestrianised, enabling the walker to view those features in relative safety.

Trocadero Restaurant,
71. St. Mary Street. Weymouth.

C. M. West, Proprietre
Telephone No. 284.

The Trocadero Restaurant

Offering the possibility of a genteel morning coffee or perhaps afternoon tea with a selection of neatly cut sandwiches and fancy cakes, the Trocadero stood at the junction of St Mary's Street and Upper St Albans Street. The Trocadero is an area of Paris across the Seine from the Eiffel Tower and was named after a battle in which the French defeated the Spanish. The name lives on in several other more glamorous catering or entertainment venues around the world.

Upper St Alban's Street

Originally known as Petticoat Lane but renamed St Albans Street, this was the upper part of the three parts of the street. The Duke of St Albans, a Georgian nobleman, is believed to have built a house close to the street. It is pleasing to note that most of the properties, which are of an interesting mixture of styles, including an Elizabethan building sadly not visible in this view, have managed to escape demolition or alteration and the street remains a popular and attractive shopping destination.

Park District

King Street

The Park District has been constructed on land reclaimed from Radipole Lake. King Street was on the edge of what was described by one health inspector as 'an extensive swamp transversed by one or two very filthy drains.' This view clearly reveals how the ground drops away from the seafront and some parts of the Park District are barely above sea level. To the left is the post office of Mr Broomfield, the publisher of many postcards. To the right, the pavement is only wide enough for one person. Tetts restaurant was a well-known tea room and popular bakery for a number of years.

Lennox Street

In this view from the early 1900s we are looking west along Lennox Street from the seafront into the Park District. This part of the seafront was known for years as 'the Narrows' because the back water and sea were only divided by this narrow strip of the sand spit that forms the seafront. All the land beyond the three-storey house adjacent to the post office was reclaimed, the intention being to create a magnificent recreational park. That plan never materialised. Instead, the densely packed residential area of the Park District was created. The house with the portico on the corner beyond the three-storey building was in fact the first house built in the development. Many of the properties became small guest houses or bed & breakfast establishments.

Derby St.

Derby Street

The project to reclaim the land for the park in the 1830s was not without its problems or controversies and was finally abandoned when the railway with its attendant tracks, sidings and station were constructed. The building of houses began in 1861, although a gale destroyed the first house early in its construction. The streets were named after Tory statesmen of the day and here we see Derby Street at its junction with Ranelagh Road. The four properties to the right carry the name Cheam Terrace.

WINDSOR TERRACE, WEYMOUTH.

Brownlow Street

The general layout of streets was agreed by the mid-1860s, but construction was random and houses and terraces were started in various places. There was no street numbering but properties were identified by names and numbers within the individual terraces. It has created an interesting street scene today, with some streets having at least two or three different building styles. That latter feature is seen in this view of Windsor Terrace, part of Brownlow Street, with two distinctly different terraces visible and the four-storey properties of Lennox Street in the distance.

Hardwick Street

This is a view of Hardwick Street, at its junction with Derby Street, from October 1908. This scene was to be repeated in July 1955. The Park District was long prone to drainage and flooding problems. It took some ninety years after the first houses were built until remedial measures finally resolved the problems. Various residents can be seen at their first-floor windows. The differing building styles of the various terraces are again apparent; the sliding gates to the right were at the entrance to a builder's yard.

The Stag Inn

The Stag Inn at the junction of Lennox Street and Walpole Street was one of several pubs in the Park District. This crossroad was the location of many shops, including a baker's, a grocer's, a greengrocer's, a haberdashery and an off-licence. Another three terraces can be seen with different architectural styles. Many of the three- and four-storey buildings were later to become small guest houses and bed and breakfast establishments. Summer evenings in this area were always busy as folk returned from the beach around five o'clock, and then again around seven as they made their way out for the evening.

Melcombe Place

Another interesting example of the fascinating differences in architectural styling that can still be seen in the Park District. In this view, we are at the junction of William Street with Melcombe Place, looking south towards Lennox Street. Two similar terraces of villas with small gardens are surrounded by railings. Sadly, the railings we see in this view were probably sacrificed for the war effort, but it is pleasing to note that today some have been replaced while others have small brick walls helping to restore much of the original charm.

Avenue Road Shopping Parade

In Avenue Road in the 1930s, the densely packed houses and smaller villas of the Park District contrast with these wider tree-lined roads of detached and semi-detached properties. The two shops visible here were part of a small parade of businesses, which included a hardware store and a chemist, in addition to those seen. The author had a paper round with the newsagents in the 1950s, then in the ownership of the Womack family. One of the boxes outside the grocer's is for Izal perforated toilet rolls.

Kirtleton Avenue

This scene of the junction between Carlton Road South and Kirtleton Avenue is dominated by a magnificently ornate street lamp. It is equalled only by the turret of the house on the corner, later to become Tower House guest house. The surrounding roads of Carlton Road, both south and north, and Glendenning Avenue were developed with large individually designed and detached properties and trees lining the pavements. The trees seen here grew into magnificent horse chestnut trees, providing an abundance of conkers for generations of small boys.

Glendenning Avenue

Glendenning Avenue, like Kirtleton Avenue, ran parallel to Dorchester Road and consisted of larger detached properties such as this one, No. 9, 'Lambourn'. At the time this picture was taken, between 1916 and 1919, it was a Red Cross hospital. St John's Hospital opened at St John's Mission House, Chelmsford Street in October 1914 and relocated to Glendenning Avenue in early 1916, finally closing three years later. In the census for 1911, the building was a private residence and shows details for seven residents, including three servants, indicating a sizeable property.

Dorchester Road

The buildings of Weymouth College can be seen to the left as we look southwards along Dorchester Road towards the area originally known as Melcombe Common, now the busy Westerhall one-way system. In 1872, as Weymouth grew and the boundaries of the town were extended, it was agreed that Dorchester Road would extend from Waterloo Place to the boundary with Radipole, presumably somewhere in the Lodmoor area. In 1897, the various terraces and parades along the road were renumbered in a continuous sequence, although it was not until later in the twentieth century that this was extended to include Upwey.

Dorchester Road

The photographer has captured a view of one of the more striking terraces along Dorchester Road opposite St Augustine's church, and is looking north towards Lodmoor Hill. It was to the rear of this terrace that the Radipole Barracks was located. A regiment of dragoons were quartered in those barracks during the visits of George III. Dragoons were originally mounted infantry but over time they evolved into light cavalry units.

Goldrings at Lodmoor Hill

Mr Goldring and his staff are pictured outside his business on Lodmoor Hill. It gives us a glimpse of neighbourhood shopping in the 1950s before the era of supermarkets and superstores. The intricate window display of products was a familiar feature for stores and there were professional window dressers who were employed to construct them. Among the products on show here are Kellogg's Corn Flakes, Sylvan soap flakes, Vim scouring powder, Lyons tea and Creamola, a fizzy drink made from flavoured crystals.

Towards Radipole Spa

Once more, we have a fascinating variety of building styles and architecture. To the left are three-storey villas, and to the right, from the junction with Fernhill Avenue, are semi-detached family homes. The workmen digging in the road have no need of traffic control as they go about their task; today, they would need traffic lights and the queue would probably stretch northwards towards the junction with Spa Road (seen in the distance and probably beyond). The boundary between the two communities of Melcombe and Radipole was regularly disputed as Weymouth and Melcombe grew and extended northwards. Agreement on a boundary was finally reached in 1835.

Upwey

SOURCE OF THE RIVER WEY WEYMOUTH.
NOW FRETTING OER A ROCK,
NOW SCARCELY MOVING THRO A REEDY POOL

Source of the River Wey

The legend reads, 'Source of the River Wey, Weymouth – now fretting oer a rock – now scarcely moving thro a reedy pool.' The spring and source of the River Wey at Upwey rises from the base of the Ridgeway stone and flows for some 4 miles to meet the sea at Weymouth. It is interesting to note the use of the phrase 'a reedy pool'; it is thought by some that Radipole is derived from these two words. Some fifty years after this tranquil scene was captured by the camera, a storm created havoc when depositing a record-breaking amount of rain for a twenty-four hour period in the UK on the higher ground above the source.

The Wishing Well

The Georgians, with their fascination for 'taking the waters', were perhaps the first to visit 'the Springs' and thus develop it as an attraction for visitors. The description of the wishing well followed the use of the name in the novel *Broken Bonds*, first published in 1874. The land owners, the Gould family, obviously had an eye for a marketing opportunity, for the name has remained and the well is still a popular attraction. The tradition was to take a sip of the water, make a wish and throw a coin into the well. The wooden shelter was replaced with a sturdier stone shelter by 1905.

Upwey Village

An idyllic rural scene of Upwey village, with thatched cottages and the church of St Laurence captured by the camera. The site of the wishing well is just out of the picture on the left. Looking at this quiet pastoral scene, it is difficult to comprehend the destruction that was unleashed from the hills at the rear of the village. A storm on 18 July 1955 deposited an amazing 9 inches of rain in this village. Nearby villages also recorded incredible levels: Martinstown recorded 11 inches, Friar Waddon 9.5 inches, and Elwell 8.3 inches. The bulk of this water flowed through Upwey, Nottington, and Radipole, then on to Weymouth, causing enormous damage. Some have estimated that an area of 200 square miles received over 5 inches of rain (or 750,000 gallons per square mile).

Upwey Mill

This mill was built in 1805 and replaced an earlier building occupied at one point by the Sprague family. They were 'fullers' by trade, cleansing and thickening cloth, and a family will details ownership of eighty sheep, forty-two lambs and four pairs of shears. They would probably have sheared their own flock and processed the wool at the mill. The family later moved to Fordington and then sailed to New England in 1628/29, helping to found Charlestown, Massachusetts. Thomas Hardy used features of this mill and another at Sutton Poyntz in his description of Overcombe Mill in his novel *The Trumpet Major*. The mill survives and is now a private residence.

Wyke Regis

The Square, Wyke Regis

Wyke Regis is one of the oldest settlements in the area. The name probably derives from the old word 'wic' or 'wick', meaning village, settlement or dwelling. The old manor of Wyke originally included Weymouth and Melcombe Regis. This view of Wyke Square is from around the early 1900s and includes, on the left, the Whitehead's Social Institute, set up for the benefit of the employees of the Whitehead's torpedo factory. The small shop on the corner in the distance is still trading.

Coastguard Cottages

Overlooking the magnificent Chesil Beach and dangerous waters of Lyme Bay, Wyke has witnessed many shipwrecks and has been used as a lookout for centuries, both to launch rescues and retrieve the bounty provided by such tragedies. Smuggling would undoubtedly have been a regular activity. The coastguard service was formed in 1822 by bringing together those various services previously employed to prevent smuggling in previous centuries. This view shows houses built for the coastguard in 1886 at Wyke. The first house to be built, in the mid-1840s, has the flag in the garden. The original coastguard clifftop patrol paths were to form the route of the South West Coast Path.

Whitehead's Torpedo Works Wyke n/r Weymouth.

Whitehead's Torpedo Works

Whitehead's torpedo works at Wyke Regis opened in the early 1890s, and was a major employer in the area for over seventy years, with a short break in the 1920s. The presence of the factory was largely responsible for the residential expansion of Wyke Regis, as the need to house the workforce was met. Clearly visible in this view is the pier used to transport torpedoes along its narrow gauge railway to boats for transport across to the firing range at Bincleaves. Occasionally, torpedoes would veer off course and on one occasion a missile came ashore at Greenhill. Portland Harbour is crowded with ships from the Royal Navy's Channel Fleet.

Portland Road

Portland Road, Wyke Regis, is the only road link to the island from the mainland. This view, looking north, is from the 1930s and you would be very lucky to see the road this deserted today. The arrival of Whitehead's torpedo factory created many jobs, and estates were constructed on either side of the road for housing. Today, the junction of Langton Road and Merley Road is located where the car is parked. Ironically, the torpedo works are no more, having been replaced by housing.

Preston & Osmington

The View from Overcombe Corner
A scene of Weymouth Bay from Overcombe before the Second World War is viewed over the chimneys of the six coastguard cottages that were close to Furzy Cliff. Thousands of years ago, the sea swept across Lodmoor as far as Radipole Lake, and the shingle bank has been formed by the action of sea and tide to act as a barrier. Lodmoor, and the amount of water seen, only emphasises just how poor the drainage is due to its low level. It is amazing to recall that Butlin's once considered building a holiday camp there. This view also shows just how vulnerable the road was to flooding, and large amounts of shingle were regularly thrown over the then low wall. The shingle drift used to build the spit originally has always been a problem, and the groynes erected to help reduce this are visible, although they soon became worn and ineffective.

Bowleaze Cove

Bowleaze Cove viewed from the base of Furzy Cliff sometime in the early 1930s. The fragile nature of the cliffs can be seen, together with the groynes and a concrete block. Both measures, it was hoped, would slow the erosion of the soft ground, although both proved ineffective. There were frequent landslips in the 1960s and 1970s, and as the cliff edge neared the coastguard cottages, seen on the previous page, four were demolished. Bowleaze Cove itself was, at the time of this photograph, still relatively undeveloped, with just a few huts lining the bank of the River Jordan as it enters the sea. To the right is Broadrock and Redcliff Point; the latter is the eastern end of the Shilvinghampton ridge, which extends from Chapel Hill at Abbotsbury to this point.

Sutton Poyntz

The Poyntz family had a manor at Sutton from the thirteenth century; the name Sutton is a combination of two Old English words, *sud* (south) and *tun* (farm). It is here that a spring rises at the base of the limestone north of the village, then joining another stream and flowing as the River Jordon to Bowleaze Cove and the sea. To meet an increasing demand for water from a rapidly expanding Weymouth, an Act of Parliament was passed to extract water from this abundant source at Sutton Poyntz. The waterworks were designed by Hawksley and the chimney for the pumping station, demolished in 1979, dominates the village in this view. The thatch on the cottages is beginning to look uncared for; the village took on a very careworn appearance for a number of years. However, the village today has a much improved appearance.

St Andrew's Church, Preston

St Andrew's church at Preston looks fine in this postcard produced by Kestins of Weymouth. The building is noted for its Norman features. Records dating from the thirteenth century indicate that the parish provided for a canon at Salisbury Cathedral, a link that remains. The name of the village is from the Old English for priest (*preost*) and farm (*tun*). Evidence of much earlier occupation in the area was revealed with the discovery of an Iron Age cemetery at Jordan Hill. Evidence of Roman occupation in the form of the foundations of a Roman temple above Bowleaze Cove can be seen today. A hoard of over 4,000 coins was also discovered at Jordan Hill in 1928, which followed an earlier find of coins in 1812.

Osmington Waterfall

Osmington has long been a 'must visit' on many visitors' itineraries, although the waterfall seen in this view is no longer as spectacular; it is yet another victim of coastal erosion. The headland in the background is at Ringstead. At West Ringstead, there are the remains of a medieval village. The presence of the coastguard station on the clifftop indicates the risk to shipping all along this coast. A barge, *The Minx*, used for coaling vessels in Portland Harbour, broke from her moorings during a storm and the gale blew her across Weymouth Bay to here at Osmington, where she foundered in the 1920s.

The White Horse

An unusual view of King George III astride the White Horse carved into the hillside above Osmington village and its church. The carving was cut in 1808 by Mr Wood, a Weymouth bookseller, and was paid for by Mr John Rainier. It is a long-held local myth that George III took offence as it depicted him riding away, and thus he vowed never to return. However, he paid his last visit to the town in 1805, some three years before the carving was completed. The road that passes the carving is today an important route into Weymouth, but it is a comparatively new road that does not appear on old maps until the eighteenth century, when a coaching route was established between Weymouth, Wareham and Poole.

Buildings, Churches & Monuments

All Saints Church, Wyke Regis
A church has stood on this spot since 1172. The building seen here was built
in 1445, and there were ancient barrows in the area indicating very early
settlements occupying the highest ground for centuries before. All Saints was
the 'mother' church for the old borough of Weymouth until Holy Trinity
was built. The churchyard has graves of the many poor souls who died in
wrecks off Chesil Beach; among them John Wordsworth, brother of the
poet William. John was the captain of *The Earl of Abergavenny.* The vessel
was sailing to Bengal and China in February 1805 with 400 passengers and
crew when she struck the Shambles while trying to make sheltered water in
Portland Roads. More than 300 souls drowned.

Belfield House, Wyke Regis

Belfield House was a magnificent Wyke mansion built by Isaac Buxton around 1780 and surrounded by 13 acres of land. The Buxtons retained ownership until the mid-nineteenth century, and eventually another large house, Portmore, known to generations of grammar school pupils as Connaught House, was built in the grounds. By the middle of the twentieth century, new housing developments grew up around the house and grounds as the owner sold off parts of the estate. The Buxtons were a wealthy family; Thomas Fowell Buxton was MP for Weymouth and was also prominent in the campaign to abolish slavery, succeeding William Wilberforce as leader of the campaign in the House of Commons.

WEYMOUTH PAVILION TEA ROOMS

The Pavilion Theatre

The Pavilion Theatre was built on reclaimed land and opened in 1908. It was constructed from wood over a steel frame, a factor that contributed to its rapid destruction by fire in 1954. It closed as a theatre for the duration of the Second World War, and became part of HMS *Bee*, as the Royal Navy's shore establishment was known. In 1943, as part of the build up to D-Day, the Americans took over operational control and it became known as the USS *Grasshopper*. The building was handed back in 1947 and renamed The Ritz. This evocative view of the tea rooms that were part of the palm court within the building captures the genteel atmosphere of the time.

MIRACULOUS CHAIR AT THE GUILDHALL WEYMOUTH
FORMERLY IN THE POSSESSION OF THE MONASTERY WEYMOUTH.

The Miraculous Chair

The friary of the Blackfriars, or Dominicans, was located in an area near Maiden Street and disappeared with the dissolution of the monasteries in 1538. Unlike many of its contemporaries, it was not a wealthy establishment, despite being involved with important commercial and welfare issues in the old borough of Melcombe. Despite this, the prior's chair survives. It was given to the friary by a cardinal and the symbols of his office, including a cardinal's hat, are carved into the chair. It was believed that anyone who died while sitting in the chair would be met by St Peter at the gates of heaven with all sins forgiven, thus guaranteeing a place in heaven. The chair was lost for a time, but was found, restored and is now held by Weymouth Museum.

Christchurch, King Street

Christchurch, at the junction of Park Street and King Street, is photographed here by Cummings, one of the many local photographers, from the car park of Weymouth station around the 1900s. The church was built and consecrated in 1874 to serve the expanding Park District as a chapel of ease to St Mary's church. Sadly, by the 1930s, congregations had diminished and closure followed in 1939. During the Second World War, it saw service as a British restaurant and was later known to a generation of school children as the Cookery Nook. The building was sold in 1955 and demolition followed. I recall walking past on my way to and from school and observing the tower being removed.

Royal Baths

Opened in 1824, the Royal Baths occupied a site that linked both St Mary's Street and St Thomas Street. This view with the Ionic columns is of the St Thomas Street side. The bather had a choice of seawater pumped directly from the bay or freshwater from the spring at Sutton Poyntz. A choice of first- or second-class baths was available; the former were of marble and provided both extra space and a 'commodious dressing room', while the latter were 'principally of porcelain'. Hot and cold shower baths, vapour and douche baths and sweating baths with warm and cold plunge baths to follow were also offered. On Saturday afternoons and evenings, the facilities were available at half price.

Convent of the Sacred Heart
The religious order of the Sacred Hearts of Jesus and Mary had its origins in the French Revolution. The order arrived in Weymouth from Trowbridge and acquired the building seen in this view in the 1890s. They used it as both a convent and what became known as the French Convent School. The correspondent, one of the nuns I believe, has marked the picture and describes it to a friend in France. This building, at the junction of Carlton Road South and North, is now in private ownership.

The New Convent of the Sacred Heart
The foundation stone of the building seen in this picture was laid in 1909 and opened in 1910 as a boarding and day school. The school closed in 1992 and the building and playing field is now housing. The convent was used, as were so many buildings in Weymouth, as a Red Cross hospital between 1914 and 1917. The convent published a whole series of postcards of the chapel, classrooms, laboratories, playing fields and dormitories to promote the school; the effort was not wasted as the institution expanded into two other buildings at Lodmoor and Glendenning Avenue.

St Paul's Church

A fine view of St Paul's church in Abbotsbury Road, Westham, photographed not long after its completion in 1913. This building replaced the chapel of ease that was opened on the opposite side of the road in 1880 to provide for the spiritual needs of Westham as it began to expand. The foundation stone for the new church was laid in 1894 by the daughter of Robert Whitehead. A new parish was created in 1901 and the completed building opened in 1913. The original chapel became the parish room. St Paul's school also opened in 1880.

St Paul's Harriers

The successful St Paul's Harriers athletes proudly display their trophies alongside the vicar, who was the founder of the church boy's club of which the Harriers were a part. The club is still thriving and a history on their website has provided the following names: (back row) F. Payne, L. Uncles, H. Young, R. Hall, C. Bartlett, T. Keech, R. Bagell, T. Bagell; (middle row) Revd M. Fisher, F. Palmer, B. Woodwood, T. Welland, S. Bridgeman, W. Barret, N. Reed, H. Shaw, E. Lovell, W. Symonds (Handicap Sec.), T. Prinhead (Hon. Sec. & Treasurer); (front row) W. Anderson, R. Brown, R. T. Wellman, G. Bugler (Capt.), C. Nes (Sub. Capt.), W. Brantingham, R. Lovell. Given the date, 1914, it is sobering to think of the possible fate of these young men in the First World War, which was about to engulf their world.

The Cenotaph

The cenotaph on Weymouth seafront was dedicated on Sunday 6 November 1921. Although this postcard is from around the 1930s, it is clear from the volume of personal wreaths laid that the sacrifice made by so many was still remembered by local folk. The memorial is constructed from Portland stone and stands almost 18 feet high. The sea and weather caused weathering to the stone and its inscriptions and replacement bronze plaques were fitted in 1932. Following the Second World War, further plaques bearing the names of those killed in that conflict were added. Today, memorials to the men of the Anzac forces from the First World War flank the cenotaph to honour those who made that long journey and fought so valiantly at Gallipolli and elsewhere.

The D-Day Memorial

Sadly, within twenty-three years of the cenotaph's dedication, Weymouth was to witness another influx of soldiers from across the ocean. The port was a major embarkation port for the US Army's First Division ('the Big Red One') in Operation Overlord, the amphibious assault on the Normandy coast of France. A total of 517,816 troops and 144,903 vehicles left Weymouth and Portland Harbours on D-Day and over the following months. The memorial of Portland Stone stands 20 feet high and the light is never switched off. It was unveiled in 1947 and a service is held there following the town's remembrance service every November.

People & Events

CLARK & ENDICOTT MEMORIAL AT WEYMOUTH. P.T

Clark Endicott Memorial

Weymouth has played a part in the development of America. In 1623, an expedition from Bradpole led by Robert Gorges settled in Wessagusset in New England, later to be renamed Weymouth. Five years later, John Endicott set sail from Weymouth in *The Abigail* to found another new settlement in North America. They arrived on 6 September at what was to become known as Salem, and others from Dorset followed to develop Massachusetts as a colony. Endicott became the first governor. Richard Clark was another to sail from Weymouth to the 'New World' aboard *The Delight* in 1538. He was shipwrecked but survived. The picture shows the unveiling of a memorial to both men on 2 June 1914 in front of the original Pavilion Theatre, where it remained until 1954, following the fire that destroyed The Ritz.

Weymouth College Rugby XV

The Weymouth College 1st Rugby XV is pictured during the Christmas term of 1924. The picture shows an interesting study of young men in a fascinating set of kit and caps with some shorts secured with what appears to be string. Weymouth College was a boys' public school, founded in 1863, which outgrew its original premises in Commercial Road and moved to new buildings on Dorchester Road in 1865. 'Old Boys' include Henry Sturmey (Sturmey Archer Cycles), Stuart Hibberd (BBC Announcer) and George Stainforth (the first man to fly at more than 400 mph). The school closed at the start of the Second World War and moved to Wellingborough. During the war it was used as the maternity unit, the one where I was born in fact, and later became a teacher training college.

The Man in the Iron Mask

Harry Bensley was the man in the iron mask. Behind this photograph, taken on the seafront at Weymouth, is a wonderful tale of Edwardian eccentricity. In a London club, two very rich men were discussing whether it would be possible for a man to walk round the world without showing his face. A wager of $100,000 was laid. Bensley, a thirty-one-year-old playboy, agreed to attempt the feat. Rules required Bensley to push a perambulator wearing an iron mask, which was not to be removed for any reason. He set off on 1 January 1908 with a pound in his pocket, a change of underwear in the pram, and had to sell picture postcards to fund his travel. He was required to visit a specified list of British towns and a further 125 towns in 18 other countries. He also had to find a wife who would marry him without a sight of his face. He was to be accompanied by one other person to see the rules were observed. The First World War intervened and he volunteered for military service, thus bringing the attempt to an end. However, he was given £4,000 as a consolation, which he gave to charity.

Weymouth Secondary School

Weymouth Secondary School became Weymouth Grammar School in 1927. In this photograph, Mr Frederick J. Babb, the headmaster, is seen with the football team. 'Freddie' Babb was a man who struggled to educate himself but finally became a teacher. He fought with and bullied the local establishment to achieve his aim of providing a school the town could be proud of. He would stride along the Esplanade in the school cadet corps uniform, complete with spurs at his heels. That the school produced so many outstanding pupils is testament to his belief and effort. When Mr Babb retired there were the official farewells, but on the last day of term, at the end of the school day, he walked alone to the railway station with his bags to join his wife in Scotland. Only Col. Linnett, his successor as head, was there to say goodbye. Mr Babb tried, unsuccessfully, to return to Weymouth in the years that followed.

Annual Corporation Service

November 1908 and the new mayor, Mr Frederick S. Smith, has been installed. This is the Corporation service on the Sunday following the council meeting at which he was elected. Before the two towns were unified, Melcombe elected a mayor in a tradition dating back to the 1300s, while Weymouth elected two bailiffs. After the union of 1571, one mayor was elected to represent both communities. At one point, the mayor was chosen on 21 September, but after 1835, with the passing of a Parliamentary Act, this moved to 9 November (except when this date fell on a Sunday). A further change in 1948 moved the date to May. In this picture, the procession has left St Mary's church and is returning to the guildhall. At the head are the aldermen, with the lighter coloured flashes to their headgear, and the mayor. Following are the councillors and other civic dignitaries.

Volunteer Firemen

The aldermen, councillors and other dignitaries have passed, and photographer Edwin Seward, having changed plates, has captured the remainder of the procession. Splendidly attired in their magnificent helmets, Weymouth's volunteer firemen are at the head of this section. To their rear, the military in the form of local volunteers are preparing to march off as the drummer takes position. The local constabulary are still in formation as the guard of honour outside the church. Beyond the church is the market hall. The former premises of Messr Gosden are standing empty. The other striking feature is the size of the crowd. Civic pride was a lot greater than today, with no television or radio to keep people at home.

Fire at the Gloucester Hotel
The Gloucester Hotel was severely damaged by fire on 3 March 1927 and this view is most probably from the day after. The extent of the destruction to the roof and first floor is clearly visible. As part of the repair work an additional floor was added. The event produced an unlikely hero in William Dicker, who was the hotel 'boots'. During the fire, onlookers were astonished to see him climb drainpipes and a parapet to rescue two elderly female guests. A detachment of Royal Marines from HMS *Tiger*, a battleship and gunnery training vessel, were sent from Portland to assist the fire brigade tackling the blaze. Health and safety regulations were unheard of in those days, as can be seen by the lack of safety barriers. It is interesting to note that in this view, as in so many others of the time, there is a man with a wheel barrow – the 1920s version of a 'white van man'.

Weymouth Fire Brigade
Gone are the wonderful helmets seen in the Corporation parade, on page 87, as the Weymouth fire brigade parade with new National Fire Service badges on their uniforms. A Parliamentary Act of 1938 created centralised control for fire services and mandated that local authorities had to provide local fire services. This parade of men and equipment, with councillors, perhaps, looking on, is outside the fire station situated in a seventeenth-century building at the corner of Maiden Street and St Edmond Street. Shortly after this parade, the fire station opened at North Quay in 1939. The glass shopfront in the background is Hurdle's, a butcher's, familir to generations of Weymouth residents. To the right is Maiden Street Methodist church, sadly just a ruin today after a serious fire.

The Boys' Brigade

The Bristol Boys' Brigade held an annual summer camp in Weymouth. Arriving by train on a Friday evening, they would form up in the station yard. Then, led by their band, they would march up King Street to the Esplanade and on to their camp site at Preston. A former member of the Bristol Brigade told me how well he remembered the camps and the enjoyment he derived from them. He told me they owned the field used for the camp, which a local farmer was allowed to use for the remainder of the year. The field was eventually sold for £1,200 on the advice of one brigade officer, a decision much regretted since. In this view from the 1930s, the brigade is marching along the seafront in front of the Gloucester Hotel to their Sunday evening church parade.

L'Arguenon Ashore on Christmas Day

The French ketch *L'Arguenon* was en route from Poole to St Malo when, to ride out a storm, she anchored in Weymouth Bay. Unfortunately, the storm was strong enough for the vessel to drag her anchors and she was driven onto the shore. Residents out for an early morning stroll on Christmas Day 1930 were met with an unexpected sight. Attempts on Boxing Day to refloat the vessel using a naval steam pinnace failed. While aground, the crew's supplies were supplemented by locals. An improvement in the weather and the removal of some of the ship's ballast resulted in a successful tow off the beach by well-known Weymouth salvage expert, Louis Basso.

A Naval Tradition

The caption to this postcard reads 'Father Neptune comes ashore on the sands at Weymouth'. This is a shore-based version of the maritime tradition known as 'crossing the line'. It was a form of initiation ceremony that was carried out on those seamen in the crew for whom this was their first time crossing the line as a ship crossed the equator. 'Pollywog', as the uninitiated were known, would be summoned to the court of King Neptune and subjected to a series of mildly unpleasant ceremonies involving eggs and shaving cream before finally being immersed in seawater. All received a certificate to mark their initiation. A similar ceremony provided by the Royal Navy was a feature of Weymouth regatta for a number of years.

The Proclamation of King George V

King Edward VII died on 6 May 1910, having reigned for just over nine years. On 11 May 1910, the mayor of Weymouth read the proclamation of his son, King George V. In this view, the mayoral party is leaving the dais set up in the shadow of another King George atop his plinth. Representatives from both the Army and Navy have formed a guard of honour, while a band from the Royal Marines is playing. Once again, the magnificent headgear worn by the volunteer fire brigade is prominent. In front of them stand the local constabulary with the corporation mace bearer waiting to lead the mayor and councillors away from the ceremony. A large crowd has gathered to witness the proclamation and the photographer has a position on a balcony of a property on Royal Terrace.

Coronation Day in Penny Street, 1953

Forty-three years after her grandfather's accession to the Crown, the country celebrates the Coronation of Elizabeth II on 2 June 1953. This is Penny Street, and like so many others a street party has been organised. Sadly, the weather intervened, as it did in London, and the tea party was hastily moved to the warehouse of Damers in Walpole Street. Once the rain had cleared, games were organised and the participants in the fancy dress competition lined up for the judges. Among those in this picture are my sister, Evelyn, and neighbours' children, including Christine Norbury, Graham Samways, Jimmy and Carol Fegan and Stephen and Jean Bennett. The gent in the background with the cap is Mr Bill McCarthy, who had his cobbler's workshop in the front room of his home at No. 30 Penny Street.

A Stolen Taxi

Nowadays, an abandoned or stolen car would attract very little interest, but in this mid-1950s photograph a large crowd of curious locals has gathered (including myself, stood nearest the camera in the check jerkin). This was a taxi believed to have been stolen by sailors, presumably to assist their return to Portland. One can only assume they were not trained navigators. This is at the top of Cassiobury Road, on what was once the northern boundary of the borough known as Black Rock and overlooking the Backwater. The extent of reclamation is clear; all the land occupied by the railway was reclaimed in the nineteenth and twentieth centuries. The signal box controls what was known as Weymouth Junction, where the railway to the harbour and Portland diverged. The locomotive is probably an auto train, also known as a 'push'n'pull' service to Dorchester.

Sailors & Soldiers

1ˢᵗ DORSET VOLUNTEER ARTILLERY. EN ROUTE ᵗ⁰ NOTHE CAMP WEYMOUTH.

Dorset Volunteer Artillery

In May 1859 the government authorised the formation of county-based volunteer forces consisting of rifle corps and artillery corps, the latter defending coastal towns. The volunteer force was liable to be called out 'in case of actual invasion, or the appearance of an enemy in force on the coast, or in case of rebellion arising in either of these emergencies'. These units were to become the Territorial Force established in 1908. In this picture, the 1st Dorset Volunteer Artillery Corps are seen on their way to the annual summer camp at Nothe Fort. The photographer is Cummings, and he is probably using a window from his studio, which was on the corner of St Thomas Street and School Street. The card is dated 1907, so this is possibly the last occasion on which the volunteers were to parade before becoming integrated as part of the Territorial Force in the following year.

Weymouth Camp

This view is also from July 1907 and is on the Nothe. This may well be the same men as seen on page 120. The Colonel is inspecting the line after the Sunday Church Parade and has attracted the attention of a group of young men resplendent in their Sunday best, complete with straw boaters. The trestle tables are perhaps ready for lunch. The card has been sent by one of the young men in the parade, as he sent it to his girlfriend at Ringwood. Itlooks as if the two military gentlement with the white sashes are about to approach the photographer.

Royal Engineers' Bridging Camp

The Royal Engineers had a bridging camp at Mudeford, near Christchurch, but logistical problems with the location and a storm that destroyed the kit and equipment led to the decision to relocate in 1927. The new site was to be the tidal lagoon of the fleet behind Chesil Beach at Wyke Regis. It opened in 1928 as a tented camp with space for 500 Royal Engineers, but was soon replaced with more permanent buildings. In this photograph, with Chesil Beach in the background, a bridge is under construction using Mk4 pontoons, which had a deck to replace earlier versions with an 'open boat' design. The trestle (roadway) is the Mk3 version and the tank about to test the bridge is a Vickers Medium tank Mk II, which remained in use until 1939. The bridging camp and the fleet were also used to test the 'bouncing bomb' used in the Dambuster raids.

Sailors Going On Leave.

Sailors on a 'Run Ashore'

A Friday afternoon and hundreds of sailors and Royal Marines pour onto the seafront from the wooden pier. All, no doubt, are looking forward to their period of shore leave. Cosens, with their fleet of paddle steamers, operated those vessels as 'Liberty boats', ferrying sailors to and from the many warships moored in Portland Roads for a number of years. By 1906, Portland Breakwater was complete and a major naval dockyard was developed at Castletown, Portland. Portland Harbour became a major base for the Channel fleet and Cosens had a formal arrangement to ferry men to and from the vessels. The railway from Portland to Weymouth would also be busy with men from the shore establishments. The social and commercial impacts on both Weymouth and Portland were significant.

SAILORS ON THE MARCH

Freedom of the Borough Parade

This parade took place on 12 May 1914 when Admiral Lord Charles William de la Poer Beresford was granted freedom of the borough. Admiral Beresford was commander of the Channel fleet at Portland from 1907 to 1909, which was one of the most senior naval commands. He was a well-known and popular character, known by the nickname 'Charlie B' and seen by many folk as the personification of 'John Bull', a view he encouraged by the presence of his pet bulldog. He failed to achieve his ambition of becoming First Lord of the Admiralty. Royal Terrace provides a magnificent backdrop to proceedings; it is seen as it was first built around 1816, with fourteen of the original eighteen properties visible complete with steps to the ground floor.

Transport

Ranelagh Road Engine Shed
Construction of Weymouth's railway station had begun in 1855 in anticipation of the railway's arrival. The latter was achieved two years later when the GWR opened its broad gauge line, the LSWR following a few weeks later. The two companies operated a joint service. The original timber and glass overall roof was part of Brunel's distinctive GWR design for the station. Carriage stock from both operating companies can be seen with those of the distinctive GWR 'chocolate and cream' livery visible in the foreground. The locomotive standing in the 'running shed' is of London & South Western design and may have just topped the tender with coal from the two wagons. To the left is a tree-lined Ranelagh Road, close to its junction with Charles Street. The spires of Christchurch in King Street and Gloucester Street Congregational church are seen in this view from around the 1930s.

Paddle Steamer Embassy

Cosens operated a fleet of paddle steamers that remain in the memory of a legion of holidaymakers who took trips aboard to Bournemouth, Swanage, Lulworth Cove and even Torquay from the mid-nineteenth century into the twentieth century. The growth of Cosens as a business and the growth of Weymouth Harbour were closely linked during that period. These adaptable vessels also acted as Liberty boats for the Royal Navy at Portland, playing an active role in service during the Second World War and also operating as salvage vessels for other ships in trouble. The link with the paddlers was broken in 1967 when the PS *Embassy*, seen here in another of Kestins' fine postcards, left the port for the last time.

St Patrick Departs for the Channel Islands

Bound for Guernsey and Jersey, the Channel Islands steam ship *St Patrick* departs Weymouth Harbour in the late 1950s. Weymouth's links with the Channel Islands had been long established before the first regular schedule services commenced in the late eighteenth century with the mail packet ships. Over the years, freight and passenger services operated from Weymouth using many different vessels both before and after nationalisation of the railway companies who operated the service. The vessel in this view was the third to carry the name St Patrick, having been launched in May 1947. She made her maiden voyage from Weymouth overnight on 3 February 1948, although she had been designed for daylight sailings. She left regular service from Weymouth in December 1964.

The Weymouth Motor Co. Ltd

The early 1920s and a group of holidaymakers prepare for a trip. I think it is safe to assume that the 'Great British Summer' has played its usual unpredictable hand, as the passengers appear to be prepared for a damp day; perhaps the retractable roof seen at the rear of the bus will be pulled into position before they leave. The charabanc was owned by the Weymouth Motor Company, a bus operator owned and set up in 1919 by Messrs Tilleys, Mr A'Court, Mr Bugler and Mr Bell, all local garage owners. They operated from a site in Edward Street. Five years later the company was sold to the National Omnibus & Transport Company, who went on to extend the original site. The site, which was rebuilt again after severe air raid damage in 1940, is still used today.

Acknowledgements

There have been many books published on the history of Weymouth and Melcombe Regis. I have been fortunate to have been able to refer to a number of those titles when researching and checking the history behind the photographs or postcards within these pages. Among these I must mention the many excellent publications from Maureen Attwooll, including those published with her colleagues Mr Jack West and Colin Pomeroy. *The Buildings of Old Weymouth* series published by Eric Ricketts gave much detail on Weymouth's architecture. Ronald Good's 1945 work, *Weyland,* was another title that provided many interesting geological details. The works of many others also provided a great deal of background, including books from Mark Ching and Ian Currie, the late Rodney Legg, Vic Mitchell and Keith Smith, Des Fry, Edward Page, Richard Clammer, Colin Caddy, George Forty, John Lucking, Brian Jackson and Ron Hill. Access to the internet and the enormous amount of information available at the click of a mouse has also proved invaluable. Thanks are also due to my wife, Phyl, for her encouragement and patience as I completed this project.

No book on the postcard and the seaside could be considered complete without including a comic postcard. This is a card published before the First World War, and its successors with their red-faced characters and suggestive innuendo were universally popular.